KEEP IT GOING!!
Bobby Fish
GO FOR IT DENNIS!
Win it again
Mike Efron
BE A WINNER
CORAL OF THE SEA
PHILIP
BUENA SUERTE
de parte de
RICARDO
TIJUANA
Best Wishes From Colorado!
Herby Richter U.S. POST OFFICE RETIRED
"FLASH"
Best of Luck
Kathy & Sean Ness
"1988"
Charlotte Way
Best of Luck
Good Luck
Millie Johnson
Kathy Deill
Mt Baldy Yatch Club
GOOD LUCK!
Carol
Good luck Pal
America Forever
John and Barb Tisdale
Julie Cheshire
Carole Aycock
Good Luck!
Betty + Jim Holmes
DANNY

AMERICA'S
CUP XXVII

As we reflect on our recent America's Cup victory, I wanted to take a moment to let all of you associated with Pepsi-Cola know just how much your support and encouragement has meant to the *Stars & Stripes* team.

This year's defense, as you know, presented us with some unusual problems — not the least of which was the fact that we were forced into it two years ahead of schedule. Nonetheless, thanks to our talented designers and crew and most important, our loyal supporters at Pepsi-Cola, we were able to keep the America's Cup here where it belongs — in America!

To show our appreciation, we have dedicated the first two pages of this book, America's Cup XXVII: The Official Record, to Pepsi-Cola. I think these pages capture the spirit of two great champions — Pepsi and the *Stars & Stripes* team. I hope you will find this book an enjoyable remembrance of America's Cup '88.

Thanks for making all of it possible!

Dennis Conner
Skipper, Stars & Stripes

Sail America Foundation for International Understanding

Postal Address: 720 Gateway Center Drive, San Diego, California, USA 92102   Dockside Address: 505 West Harbor Drive, San Diego, California, USA 92101
Telephone (619) 293-7220, Fax (619) 293-7240

A SALUTE TO THE CHAMPIONS...

America's Cup
XXVII

Stars & Stripes

The Official Record
1988

Dennis Conner

Publisher

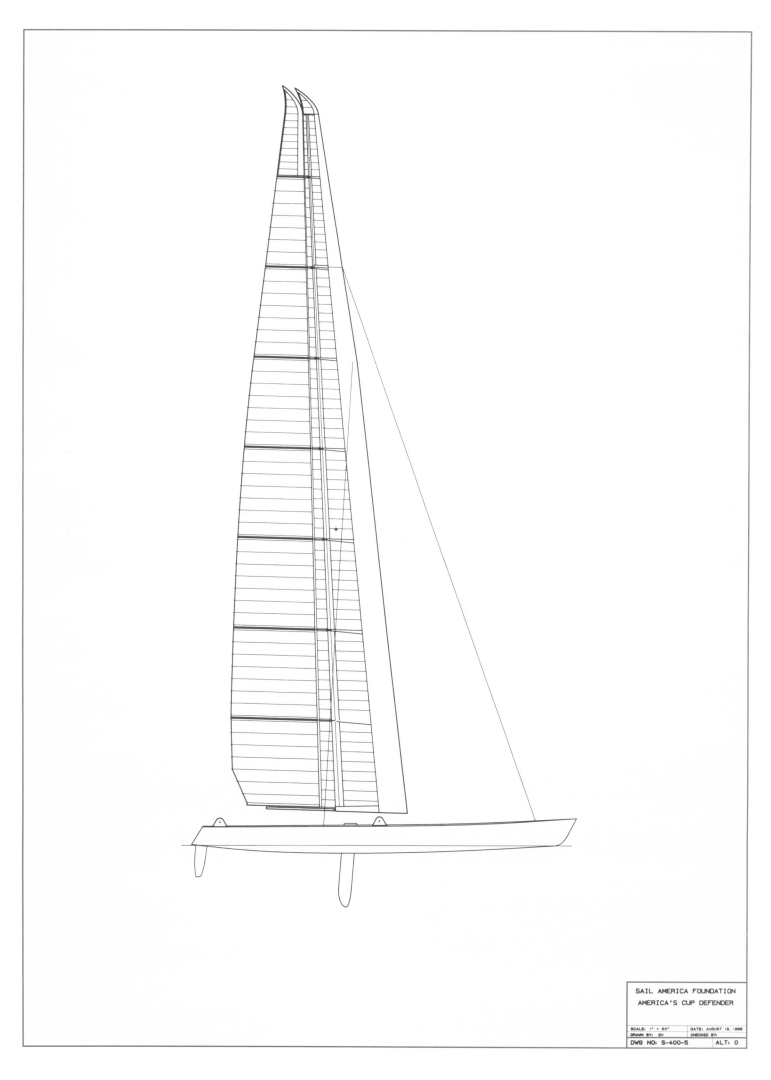

SAIL AMERICA FOUNDATION
AMERICA'S CUP DEFENDER

SCALE: 1" = 60"	DATE: AUGUST 19, 1986
DRAWN BY: EH	CHECKED BY:
DWG NO: S-400-5	ALT: 0

BRUCE FARR® AND ASSOC., INC.

P.O. BOX 3457, ANNAPOLIS, MD. 21403, U.S.A

New Zealand Challenge '88

FOR -

SCALE 1:100	DESIGN NO. 196
TITLE Rig & Sail Plan	COPYRIGHT Aug 31 1988 © BRUCE FARR® & ASSOC., INC.
CHECKED DGR	DRAWING NO.

America's Cup
XXVII

Stars & Stripes

The Official Record
1988

editor/writer
Roger Vaughan

art direction/design
Barry Feinstein

photography
Margherita Bottini
Daniel Forster
Marshall Harrington

DENNIS CONNER SPORTS, INC.
SAN DIEGO

Copyright ©1988 Dennis Conner Sports, Inc.

Grateful acknowledgement is made for permis-
sion to reprint the photographs of Margherita
Bottini, Daniel Forster, Marshall Harrington, and
those of other contributors listed on page 144.

First published by:
Dennis Conner Sports, Inc.
720 Gateway Center Drive
San Diego, CA 92102 USA

ISBN 0-9618799-1-2

Library of Congress Catalog Card Number: 88-92335

Printed in the United States of America

First Edition

Printed by Southern California Lithographics

Contents

COMEBACK 10

TRUSTEESHIP 18

CHALLENGE 28

START-UP 40

TESTING 68

SPONSORSHIP 76

WINGS 82

SAILING 96

JUDGEMENT 120

RACING 126

PARTICIPANTS 143

CREDITS 144

COMEBACK

*Dennis Conner aboard the 12 Meter LIBERTY,
now owned by D.C. Sports, Inc.*

The winning of the America's Cup in 1987 by Dennis Conner and the Stars & Stripes crew was one of those sports comebacks that make the spine tingle. The long trek through 12 time zones to Fremantle, Western Australia, and solving the logistical problems generated by two 12 Meters and rigs, chase boats, tenders, 100 or so people, and several containers full of gear, sails, and tools, was a mammoth undertaking. Before the project could even begin, millions of dollars had to be raised to support the effort. And to make it even more interesting, the pressure was intense. The whole world was watching.

In 1980, Conner & Company had come roaring out of San Diego with two hot boats and a campaign so polished, so well-organized and staffed, and so well-funded that there was no question this freshman contender would be selected to defend and win the Cup. Conner admitted to having personally sailed an average of 300 days a year for two years in preparation for the event. Other sailors, including defending champion Ted Turner, grumbled and accused Conner of becoming a professional. Conner shrugged and said he was simply doing what was necessary to win. "And unless I am mistaken," he said in his matter-of-fact way, "winning *is* the object."

Winning was something that America's Cup participants and watchers had come to take for granted. Since the schooner *America* had started the game with her defeat of the British in 1851, America had never come close to losing the Cup. As the match of 1983 began, the U.S. boasted a 132-year string of consecutive victories, most of them lopsided. It was the longest winning streak in sports. That record, and the myth of gentility under which Cup activities had been conducted over the years, no doubt prompted the criticism of what looked like Conner's overkill.

Upon examination, however, one discovers that the gentility in most Cup contests went no further than the proper attire. The America's Cup has been a contentious event since its inception. *America* failed to round the Nab lightship in 1851, its skipper claiming he didn't realize it was a mark of the course. The British let it pass. But as the years went on, there were unpleasant altercations over everything from centerboards and sliding keels to the nature of the racing rules. The most renowned disagreement was in 1895, when the British Lord Dunraven accused the U.S. of cheating, and threatened to take legal action because of the spectator wake which he said was aimed at his vessel. In 1970, the Australian parliament threatened to break off diplomatic relations with the U.S. after *Gretel II* was disqualified for a starting infraction. And in 1980 the controversy was over *Australia*'s bendy mast tip which allowed for enormous roach in the mainsail.

Then, in 1983, the unthinkable happened: we lost the Cup. The Australians arrived with a faster boat and beat *Liberty*, sailed by Conner and crew, in an exciting match that was carried live on television for the first time. Conner got well-deserved credit for staying as close to the Aussies as he did, extending the series to a seventh "Race of the Century". But the loss was a bitter pill for the man whose main sustenance is winning.

"Most people had a sense the Cup would be lost that summer," Conner says today. "That's why the press descended upon Newport, R.I. in droves during the last weeks. They have a nose for trouble. They came like they go to Indianapolis. They smelled blood on the water. They knew I was dead. They just wanted to see the accident. But the lesson for me was that out of the darkest hours can come the best in the world if you have the right attitude. I would have had a hard time in 1983 believing the loss was the best thing that ever happened to me. It's a lot easier believing that now."

Flashback: under tow on Gage Roads. STARS AND STRIPES (below)
takes water in heavy air. Overleaf, STARS & STRIPES and KIWI
MAGIC battle in the final elimination series of the 1987 Cup.

Moët champagne is broken out after the final race with Kookaburra. To the delight of spectators, Stars & Stripes sailed into the congested harbor.

In defeat, Conner was not treated with compassion. He and his crew were ignored by the New York Yacht Club to the extent that they were excluded from the trophy presentation. And when Conner arrived home in San Diego, no official greeting party awaited him on the tarmac. For he had not just lost a sailing trophy; he had lost sailing's holy grail.

But Dennis Conner is an ultimate competitor. A scant year later he announced his intention to enter the Cup arena once again, even if that arena was now half way around the world. He approached the New York Yacht Club, but they were not interested in his proposal. So he arranged to sail under the burgee of the San Diego Yacht Club, where he was a former commodore.

Malin Burnham, prominent San Diego sailor and businessman, and a long-time friend of Conner, first got involved in the America's Cup with the Enterprise campaign of 1977. By the end of that campaign, Burnham had been named skipper of the boat. In 1980 and 1983, Burnham was a backer of Conner's syndicate, and frequent helmsman of the trial horse. And it was Burnham who took the lead on the management side as Conner's Australian challenge took shape in 1984. It didn't look promising. As Burnham recalls, "We called a press conference at the swimming pool of the San Diego Yacht Club to announce our campaign. Ten people showed up."

Little financial support materialized from the local citizenry. But Fritz and Lucy Jewett, who had backed Conner in 1980 and 1983, displayed continued faith in Conner's ability to win. Mike Dingman, a financial whiz who is CEO of the multi-national Henley Group, contributed both financial support and expertise when it looked like the project might falter. And Malin Burnham gave freely of his time, money, and signature to meet a budget that would soar to $16 million. Through dogged effort, hundreds of thousands of miles traveled, endless leads checked out and potential sponsors cultivated, the campaign gained strength.

As the work progressed, it became evident that the 1983 defeat had kindled a ground swell of patriotic concern throughout the country. Even landlocked mid-

Finally, it was time to celebrate.

Westerners knew we had lost something that had been in the family for years. Whatever it was, we had to get it back. Marketing experts sensed the mood. ESPN purchased the rights to televise the Cup in the U.S., even though the races wouldn't start until midnight on the East Coast. Suddenly sponsorship became a viable commodity as the Cup attained media-event status.

The story is familiar of how Stars & Stripes set up a training camp in Hawaii, a locale of reliably heavy winds relatively close to home. Conner raised eyebrows when he chose to ignore the 1986, 12 Meter Worlds in Fremantle in favor of sustained testing against his own boats. Then came the long season in Fremantle, where if the 25-knot Fremantle Doctor and accompanying green seas didn't knock you down, the rival public relations campaigns or the media would. After sailing slightly off the pace through two round robins, Conner and crew peaked at the right time, winning the final series from the front-running New Zealanders. After three years of sustained determination, a ton of money, five new boats, and an elimination series of nearly 50 races, Stars & Stripes had won the right to challenge. The Cup itself was a typical anti-climax: Stars & Stripes, 4; Kookaburra, 0. Finally, it was time to celebrate. It had been a tireless effort, a great win on the road under the most trying circumstances.

The Kiwis registered the most shock over the outcome. They had enjoyed a phenomenal Cup season. Going into the Challenger Finals they had a won-lost record of 38-1, the best in 12 Meter Cup history. The great success of Kiwi Magic had stirred the hopes of tiny New Zealand. Hundreds of letters poured into the camp every day from well-wishers at home, and a huge percentage of New Zealand's population donated to the financial success of the campaign.

A tired but happy Conner with the Cup.

Skipper Chris Dickson, barely 24, had handled himself like a veteran both on the race course and under the harsh lights of the daily press conferences—especially when Conner and Company challenged the legality of New Zealand's fiberglass boats. Dickson and crew were feeling strong, confident, and with good reason. Then, on the verge of winning it all, Stars & Stripes had steamrollered them four races to one.

"It was no contest," said Michael Fay, the merchant banker who was syndicate boss for New Zealand. "Dennis Conner and Malin Burnham did an excellent job turning the world upside down on us. They were relentless in the way they attacked us before the series. Then Dennis went right out and sailed by us when we were testing. That had never been done before. We were a little rattled, and they seized every opportunity. Well, I learned something from that."

Exactly what Fay learned would be evident all too soon.

A satisfied Malin Burnham with the Cup.

*"Dennis Conner and Malin Burnham
did an excellent job of turning the
world upside down on us."*

Michael Fay

TRUSTEESHIP

"The New York Yacht Club, the holder of the America's Cup for most of its history, prevented the type of unwelcome challenge that now faces the San Diego Yacht Club by following the practice of issuing an announcement during the course of a match that if it was successful in defending the Cup, it would hold the next race at a certain time . . . and at a certain place... The club would also announce that the match would be sailed in 12 Meters and that all challenges received by a given date would be treated as received simultaneously. By following that practice, the New York Yacht Club and later the Royal Perth Yacht Club managed to prevent preemption of the field by one challenger.

Here, rather than issuing a statement of intent before it won or even shortly after, the San Diego Yacht Club was apparently delayed by disagreements with its contractual agent for the defense of the Cup, Sail America, about how the defense should be handled."

Supreme Court of the State of New York
dated November 25, 1987
(signed) Carmen Beauchamp Ciparick, J.S.C.

In 1985, as he was masterminding the Stars & Stripes challenge for the America's Cup in Australia, Malin Burnham had the temerity to ask himself this question: What happens if we win? From his involvement with three previous Cup matches, Burnham had developed a vision of the future, and it looked complex. His early glimpses of the monstrous effort being mounted in Western Australia—including a government expenditure of more than $50 million for waterfront and civic renovation—made him realize that the comparatively sedate Cup summers of Newport, R.I., were gone forever. The Cup had turned pro.

Future management of an America's Cup Defense would demand people with up-to-date, hands-on expertise and an international perspective. And so Malin Burnham took steps to formalize The Sail America Foundation for International Understanding's role with the San Diego Yacht Club. (At the time, Sail America was both Stars & Stripes Syndicate and the Foundation.) The particulars were cast in an eight-page "Agreement" dated September 1, 1985, that covered management of the 1987 challenge; management of America's Cup defenses in general; and licensing and promotional activities.

Malin Burnham, president of the Sail America Foundation, keeps watch on the Harbor from his office.

Overleaf: looking south across the Harbor toward the city, with the Yacht Club in the foreground.

"The San Diego Yacht Club had a bad case of seller's remorse. They thought they had given away too much to Sail America."

"It was a good agreement," Burnham says today, "but it didn't go far enough. We simply didn't know in 1985 exactly what we might get into. But several things were clear.

"The Yacht Club was concerned about the financial responsibility of being custodian of the Cup if we should win. We said OK, we understand. Sail America will guarantee that you will not have to bear the cost of being trustee. But you have to give us marketing rights so we can raise money. We'll pay the bills and provide extra security."

Current San Diego Yacht Club Commodore C. Douglas Alford, an attorney, is the man who drafted the agreement. "It was the first time before an America's Cup match that an attempt was made to set down in black and white an agreement of what would happen in the event we won," Alford says. "Of course America had never been challenger before. It was a clean-slate contract that attempted to foresee future problems. If we sat down today to write it, it wouldn't be the same. But we did alright."

With agreement in hand, Sail America raised the necessary funds and brought the 1987 Challenge up to speed. Everything went smoothly until the Stars & Stripes team returned victorious with the Cup. The first note of discord was struck when Burnham arranged to have the Cup placed in the vault of a local bank upon its arrival in San Diego. "I didn't quite know what to do with it," Burnham says today. "The Yacht Club didn't have the necessary security. So I called a banker friend who offered a substantial donation in exchange for the display of the Cup at his bank, and the use of his vault at night for a six-month period. I was told by the Yacht Club that I had overstepped my bounds."

From that point on, the relationship between Sail America and the San Diego Yacht Club deteriorated. As Burnham says, "The San Diego Yacht Club had a case of seller's remorse. They thought they had given away too much to Sail America. Success has many mothers and fathers. That's human nature. Suddenly they were speaking of the great victory 'we' had in Fremantle. It wasn't 'we' when Dennis Conner and I were standing alone in 1984, with me guaranteeing bank loans to

get us started. Less than 3% of our $16 million budget came from members of the San Diego Yacht Club."

Chief among the issues under contention was the make-up of the America's Cup Committee, which was charged (under the Agreement) with selecting the defending yacht; establishing aesthetic standards for marketing the Cup; and most important of all, determining the timing and site of the next defense. Conditions for membership in the Committee were carefully outlined in the agreement, as was the nominating and selection process. But when the Yacht Club learned that Burnham was not automatically favoring San Diego as the site, Cup Committee membership became a crucial issue. When Dennis Conner remarked in a speech to the San Diego Press Club that he favored Hawaii, concern approached panic.

Burnham (and Sail America), who by agreement had nominating rights to Committee membership, was eager to create a Committee rich with previous America's Cup administrative experience. He wanted to include world class sailors with broad perspectives, and people with event-marketing experience. "We needed to project that everything would be run fairly in order to attract entries," Burnham says. "If it was going to be a cozy, Point Loma group, there would be no competition. And there were marketing considerations. We had to have a balanced Committee."

The San Diego Yacht Club didn't want to hear about marketing. Founded in 1886, the Club is one of America's more impressive yachting establishments. Flag membership is limited to 1100. It's a proper club with tight security at the front gate. And when a Past Commodore shows up for lunch, the alert waitress quickly places a small "Commodore" flag on his table.

The large, handsome clubhouse was rebuilt only a few years ago, and the 700-odd slips are newer still. But the pride of longevity is evident everywhere on the immaculate grounds. The cover of the centennial pamphlet published by the Club in 1985 is graced by an old, gaff-rigged ketch under sail above the words, "A Century of Tradition."

The Club has a lot to be proud of. San Diego sailors have always been prominent on the international rac-

Frederick A. Frye, M.D., Commodore,
San Diego Yacht Club, 1987.

ing scene. The 1937 Star World Champion came from the S.D.Y.C., and in the glittering trophy cases that line the Club's main hallway, most of the world's major races are represented. One large photograph hanging just outside the bar brings the visitor to a halt. Pictured are three members of the Club posing with trophies they won in 1987: John Driscoll with the enormous Lipton Cup; Vince Brun with the Star Worlds trophy; and Dennis Conner with the America's Cup. Not a bad year for the San Diego Yacht Club. (Club sailors have won two of eight slots on the 1988 Olympic team.)

It was no surprise when a press release issued by the Club's board of directors in June, 1987, reflected adherence to traditional standards as upheld by the Deed of Gift: "For one hundred years the America's Cup has been a race between the world's yacht clubs. The America's Cup race is not a professional sport run for financial gain; it is a contest between the world's yacht clubs, the world's fastest 12 Meter yachts, and the world's best sailors."

And there was the matter of a site. It may have seemed strange to read in the press that staunch San Diegan Malin Burnham, with local business interests of his own, wanted to consider bodies of water other than the Pacific Ocean off Point Loma. But there was a rationale behind his apparent spate of disloyalty.

"When Dennis and I crossed the country in 1984 trying to raise money," Burnham says, "we were often asked—'If we give you a donation, will you consider holding the event here if you win?' We said we couldn't guarantee anything, but we would consider it. Then, in 1986, after we picked Hawaii as a training site, and the Cup became so popular, Hawaii got interested. So that was one thing. We had an obligation to the rest of the country to do what was best for the Cup.

"Another was my unwillingness to go out on the financial limb once again, personally. If San Diego wanted the event, I had to be assured of the City's support up front. It was my dream to have the Cup here in San Diego, but I couldn't come out and say that. I needed the Port District to say they would provide waterfront facilities. I needed a meaningful financial pledge

from the private sector. I needed a political commitment from the Mayor. I wanted all this *before* the Cup was awarded to San Diego. Otherwise, I knew I would never get it.

"Sail America wanted to defend the Cup successfully; the San Diego Yacht Club wanted to defend the Cup successfully in San Diego. That was our difference."

Frederick Frye, M.D., a pediatrician who was commodore in 1987 says he couldn't believe his ears when Burnham announced at a press conference that the Cup defense might not be in San Diego. "I had never even considered that it wouldn't be in San Diego," Frye says. "If you won the Cup, you held it at your home club. That was that. When the press called and asked for a comment on Malin's remark, I played dumb. I didn't know what game Malin was playing."

Frye found out eventually, but he and other club members maintain that Burnham's "game" got away from him. The pressure from other interested locales—especially Hawaii—was intense, with seven- and eight-figure numbers being dangled as incentive. Other areas spent big money on video presentations, and sent proposals over the signatures of high government officials. The Yacht Club and the city felt the Cup was in serious danger of being sold to the highest bidder. Burnham is one of San Diego's more powerful and respected citizens, a wealthy man known for his tough business posture. But as the venue question was played out, the attack on him in the local media reached vicious proportions. Both sides were firmly entrenched with their respective arguments. In another press release, the Yacht Club stated: "The issue is not which venue is considered by the media, advertising, or television to be the most interesting or exciting, or the 'best.' This 'media' debate misses the point."

The Yacht Club's tenacity was admirable. But alas, it is naive to espouse Corinthian ideals in the face of what an event like the America's Cup costs to produce. For such an event, media/marketing influence is inevitable. Just as artificial turf has replaced stadium grass, television time-outs and official replays have become a part of big-time football, and race cars are plastered with corporate logos, so the America's

"The America's Cup race is not a professional sport run for financial gain."

Douglas C. Alford, Commodore,
San Diego Yacht Club, 1988.

Cup had to seek sponsorship to survive. Because the Cup has gotten that big—that expensive to challenge for, or defend. Western Australia reported a Cup-related gross of almost $700 million from the 1987 event. A study by CIC Research, Inc., done for San Diego's America's Cup Task Force, predicted that the 1991 event would add $1.2 billion to San Diego's economy.

As *The San Diego Union*'s Tom Coat wrote in July, 1987, "The expertise (for managing a Cup defense or challenge) has shifted (from the yacht clubs) to the syndicates. Conner and Malin Burnham...say they have the expertise to put on a modern America's Cup. And, perhaps as importantly, they have the name recognition to go out into the corporate world and raise the millions needed for campaigns and for the staging of a proper regatta. Conner, Stars & Stripes, Sail America—each commands attention in board rooms. . . ."

Several months passed while the inter-fraternal dispute raged in San Diego. Stirrings of unrest were heard in the America's Cup community both here and abroad. Paranoia—always lurking beneath the surface of international competition—raised its ugly head: what was San Diego up to? What sort of foul play was going on regarding the future of the Cup? What was, in truth, a family squabble took on whatever ominous undertones one wished.

The conflict finally came to binding arbitration, a resolution one new board member still finds hard to believe. "It's just amazing that people couldn't sit down and solve the problem. But I don't think the board was able to stand up to Malin personally. He's a very intimidating guy. So they did it legally."

The specific issue was the membership of the America's Cup Committee that would select the site. In appointing the Committee, the San Diego Yacht Club Board of Directors had ignored the sailing personalities nominated by Sail America in favor of sailors with a San Diego address.

On June 19, 1987, after hearing five days of testimony and deliberating for three days, retired Superior Court Judge Charles W. Froehlich, Jr., made a ruling that effectively disbanded the Committee. Sail America was instructed to resubmit its nominations.

The new Committee agreed upon included Gene Trepte, a former SDYC commodore who had helped form the first West Coast Cup bid in 1962 with *Columbia*; Kim Fletcher, head of San Diego's Home Federal Savings & Loan Association and a world class Star sailor; Gerry Driscoll, a San Diego boat builder who, as skipper of *Intrepid*, narrowly missed being selected to defend the Cup in 1974; Charles D. Hope, architect and past S.D.Y.C. commodore who has co-owned several race boats with Conner; John Marshall, head of the Stars & Stripes design team in 1987 (and mainsail trimmer on *Liberty* in 1983) and Sail America trustee; Harry L. Usher, past Executive Vice President and General Manager of the Los Angeles Olympic Committee; and Gary Jobson, tactician aboard Cup winner *Courageous* in 1977, ESPN-TV commentator in 1987, and sailing consultant.

It had been a difficult few months in San Diego as a raft of third-generation San Diegans found themselves polarized by an emotional issue. Froehlich's decision cleared the way for progress, but it wouldn't immediately erase the lingering bitterness, or mend the many relationships within San Diego's yachting community that had been strained.

"Our argument with Sail America was vociferous," Doug Alford says with a wry smile, "but since arbitration, I think we have taken the team approach. I was on the leading edge of Yacht Club representation, but I've been pragmatic about the outcome. Perhaps that's because of my gray hairs, and that as an attorney I am used to disputes. But mainly we had to work together to defeat a common enemy. There are some continuing disagreements between certain individuals—there are a few people you don't invite to the same party—and perhaps there is a degree of cynicism about people's motives that didn't exist before. Maybe that's healthy."

Even after arbitration, things moved with underlying reluctance. The new America's Cup Committee was not officially announced until July 25, more than four weeks later. By then it was too late. Eight days earlier, on July 17, Michael Fay had arrived with a challenge that would alter Cup history.

TRUSTEESHIP
Malin Burnham

Malin Burnham at the helm of the 12 Meter Enterprise.

Malin Burnham began racing seriously when he was 10 years old. His boat was a Starlet, a San Diego Yacht Club junior class similar to a Star boat. The boat was smaller overall, with a shorter mast and a longer boom. Starlets have since disappeared from the San Diego scene.

Burnham moved up to a Star at the age of 15, crewing for Gerry Driscoll in 1944 when Driscoll won the Star World Championships. Two years later, as skipper, Burnham won the Star Worlds himself. At 17, he was the youngest ever to win the Star Worlds, a record that should stand for a long time. His crew: Lowell North, age 15, who would go on to found North Sails. Burnham actively raced Stars until 1979. That year he accepted the presidency of the class, serving in that capacity until 1983.

Burnham has been active on the international ocean racing circuit all his life. He has been San Diego Fleet Champion, and has won the San Diego Lipton Cup four times, and the San Francisco Perpetual Trophy three times.

He skippered Enterprise during the 1977 Defender Trials, and was practice helmsman during the 1980 (Freedom), and 1983 (Liberty) Cup campaigns. He became President of the Sail America Foundation for the 1987 Challenge.

Malin Burnham is Chairman of John Burnham & Company, which was founded in 1891 by his grandfather as a real estate business. When Malin became President in 1962, the company had 11 employees. Today the John Burnham Company has 323 employees, and is involved in real estate, real estate management, commercial and personal insurance, and real estate finance.

Burnham is Chairman of Burnham Pacific Properties, Inc., and Burnham American Properties, Inc. He is a Director of the First National Bank; San Diego Gas & Electric Co.; Cubic Corporation; Gen-Probe, Inc.; and the Businessmen's Assurance Company of America.

He is a member of the San Diego Realty Board; San Diego Mortgage Bankers Association; California Mortgage Bankers Association.

He is a Director of the San Diego Hall of Champions; Greater San Diego Sports Association; and San Diegans, Inc.

He is a Trustee of Stanford University, and Chairman of La Jolla Cancer Research Foundation.

Burnham is Past Commodore of the San Diego Yacht Club, and holds memberships in the St. Francis and New York Yacht Clubs.

CHALLENGE

Syndicate boss Michael Fay on the afterdeck of the New Zealand challenger.

Doug Alford first met Michael Fay in Sardinia during the 12 Meter World Championships held in June of 1987. "He asked me," Alford recalls, "if we had set the date for the next America's Cup. The arbitration decision had just been made. I received the news in Sardinia. I told Fay that when we got home, we would get things going."

The 1987 Worlds were a high point for Michael Fay. New Zealand won the regatta against a line-up of talented teams that included Dennis Conner and his *Stars & Stripes* crew. Fay was an active participant in the 12 Meter Association Owners Committee meeting held to discuss marketing for the 1991 Cup match that was being planned for San Diego.

On the way home from Sardinia, Fay and his attorney Andrew Johns stopped in New York on business, then flew to San Diego.

"I rang up Commodore Frye," Michael Fay says, "and he invited Andrew and myself to lunch at the San Diego Yacht Club the next day. Over lunch I told Frye and Vice Commodore Alford that we were looking forward to having another go at the Cup. They said they'd be delighted to see the Kiwis again. I explained we would be coming sooner than 1991. They raised their eyebrows. I said we would be coming in a bigger boat—a 90-footer."

Sitting on the sunny deck of the Yacht Club, Doug Alford recalled the Fay luncheon. "Fred Frye was late for lunch, which frequently happens because he's a doctor. So I greeted Fay and Johns, and right off they said they had a challenge they wanted to deliver after lunch in a boat with a 90-foot waterline. I was somewhat stunned. I didn't know what to say. But what came right off the top of my head was this: 'I guess we can respond in a 90-foot catamaran.'" Alford says that Fay and Johns didn't react to what was an amazingly prophetic remark.

Dr. Fred Frye has a clear memory of that day as well. "It was a congenial luncheon. We spoke about the 12 Meter World Championships, the formation of the America's Cup Committee. Then over coffee they spelled it out: Mercury Bay Boating Club would challenge us in a 90-foot waterline boat in June of 1988. I listened knowing immediately that they had found a loophole. I knew they had done their homework and figured they could do what they said or they wouldn't be here. I knew inside it was a valid challenge, although I didn't reveal that. I didn't know Fay, but I knew Andrew Johns to be a bright young man who would not go off half-cocked."

Alford: "I told them we would 'take them under submission,' a phrase a judge uses to accept an argument for consideration. Then we shook hands and they left."

Fay and Johns had left Auckland together for the 1987 World 12 Meter Championships in Sardinia. Not every

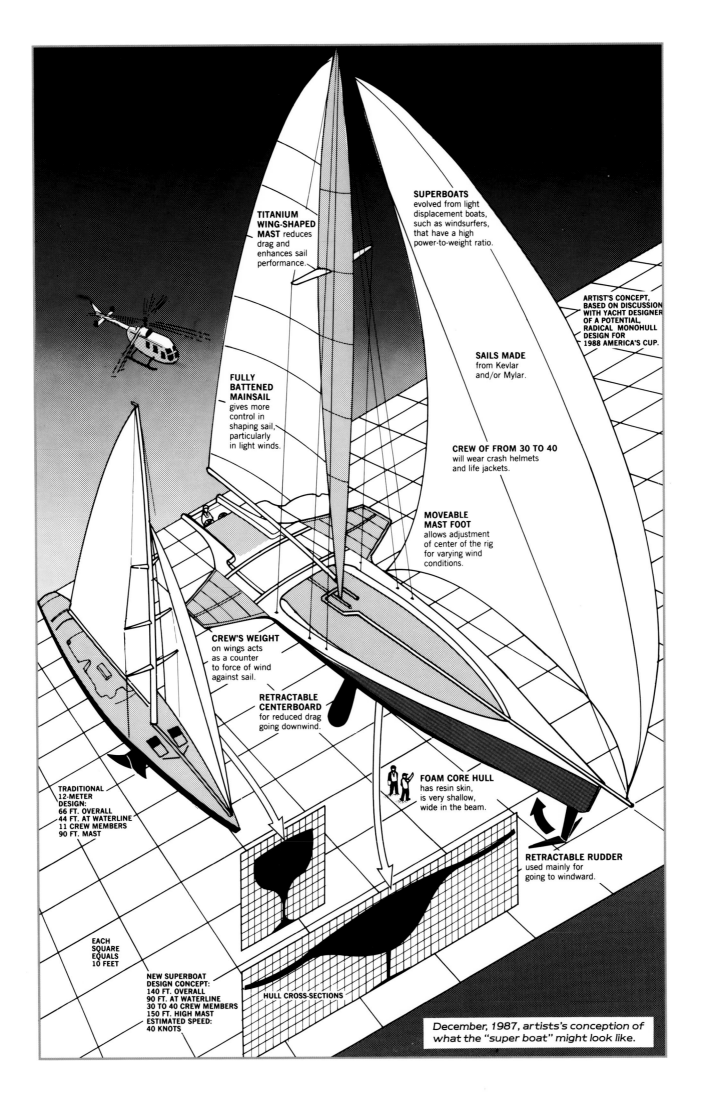

TITANIUM
WING-SHAPED
MAST reduces
drag and
enhances sail
performance.

SUPERBOATS
evolved from light
displacement boats,
such as windsurfers,
that have a high
power-to-weight ratio.

ARTIST'S CONCEPT,
BASED ON DISCUSSION
WITH YACHT DESIGNER
OF A POTENTIAL,
RADICAL MONOHULL
DESIGN FOR
1988 AMERICA'S CUP.

FULLY
BATTENED
MAINSAIL
gives more
control in
shaping sail,
particularly
in light winds.

SAILS MADE
from Kevlar
and/or Mylar.

CREW OF FROM 30 TO 40
will wear crash helmets
and life jackets.

MOVEABLE
MAST FOOT
allows adjustment
of center of the rig
for varying wind
conditions.

CREW'S WEIGHT
on wings acts
as a counter
to force of wind
against sail.

RETRACTABLE
CENTERBOARD
for reduced drag
going downwind.

FOAM CORE HULL
has resin skin,
is very shallow,
wide in the beam.

TRADITIONAL
12-METER
DESIGN:
66 FT. OVERALL
44 FT. AT WATERLINE
11 CREW MEMBERS
90 FT. MAST

RETRACTABLE RUDDER
used mainly for
going to windward.

EACH
SQUARE
EQUALS
10 FEET

NEW SUPERBOAT
DESIGN CONCEPT:
140 FT. OVERALL
90 FT. AT WATERLINE
30 TO 40 CREW MEMBERS
150 FT. HIGH MAST
ESTIMATED SPEED:
40 KNOTS

HULL CROSS-SECTIONS

December, 1987, artists's conception of
what the "super boat" might look like.

New Zealand is christened in Auckland on March 27, 1988, amid a throng of well-wishers. Below, looking like several cricket teams that have escaped the pitch, the crew of 36 examines the deck that measures 26 feet wing-to-wing.

The big boat out of water: a 130-footer with the underbody of a radical, 40-foot Lake Garda boat. The curves are sumptuous, the finish like a mirror. The fear that the built-in hiking racks would catch water was unfounded.

raceboat owner brings his attorney to regattas, but Fay says Johns is his "rules expert," the guy who keeps his eye on things and interprets the sailing instructions. Fay says he and Johns had talked a lot about the Cup in Fremantle after the U.S. won. "We would challenge, that was certain," Fay says. "We had been to a lot of 12 Meter Association meetings together, and we had a common frustration about the way things were handled. Our philosophy about the Cup was in tune. So it was no surprise when Johns came to me early in June, 1987, and said he had some thoughts about a Cup challenge that he wanted to put in front of me. Something other than the 12 Meter format."

Fay says he was busy at the time, and asked Johns to put his ideas on paper. "On June 12 or 14, I forget the exact date, Johns handed me his ideas on the subject. I called in Richwhite (Fay's business partner) and we spent about 15 minutes on it. The Deed clearly specified challenger-initiation. It could be sooner than later, and it wouldn't have to be in 12 Meters. It looked fine in principal. Of course it would have to be checked out."

Fay says Johns left Sardinia supposedly for London to do Fay, Richwhite & Company business. In fact, Fay sent Johns to New York to confer with another Fay attorney, George Tompkins, to solidify his interpretation of the Deed. While there he did additional research on the 90-footer challenge he had proposed. So while Fay was in Sardinia being a loyal, hard-working member of the 12 Meter Association, his attorney was plowing through America's Cup records in the New York Public Library, and in the library of the New York Yacht Club, preparing his America's Cup bomb.

During the marketing session of the 12 Meter Class meetings in Sardinia, Fay carried on about the commercial value of the America's Cup. "I'm told he gave the impression," says Frye with a smile, "that he thought the commercialization was awful, but he'd handle it differently and make even more with it." It was what Malin Burnham observed as Fay's Sardinian Sting that caused

him to be so outraged at news of the challenge.

"After our luncheon in San Diego," Frye says, "I called Malin. 'I think we have a problem—we've just been challenged in a boat with a 90-foot waterline.' Malin's first several words were expletives best deleted. Then he said 'No way!' The next day he told the press he thought Fay was a madman."

Fay and Johns flew back to New Zealand and waited for a response. There was nothing. "When lunch came to an end," Fay says, "they said, 'We'll be in touch.' They never were. We finally sent them a letter: 'Could we have the courtesy of a reply, please?' We got nothing. We put the challenge down, we got no response, so we had no recourse. We had to go to court. I don't have any apologies for going to court. If you believe in the issue and believe you're right, that's what you have to do."

In hindsight, Fred Frye sees one avenue that might have worked. "I had a two to three week window," he says, "before Fay started building the boat when I could have gone to him. I could have said 'OK, let's jump into the 20th century, but not in a 90-footer. Let's do it in a boat we can all play in.' I might have been able to sell that. But first of all, I can't speak unilaterally for the Club. The Board would have had to vote, and that would take time. And if I had done that, it would have violated our contract with Sail America Foundation, and Malin would have sued us in a minute."

Michael Fay was at least notified in the San Diego newspapers, which ranked his challenge third most newsworthy item behind the naming of the America's Cup Committee, and the appointment of Thomas F. Ehman, Jr., as Executive Vice President and Chief Operating Officer of Sail America. Local journalists concluded that the New Zealand Challenge could well be forgotten once "the big picture"—the 1991 Cup Defense—came into sharper focus.

Sail America moved ahead on two fronts. They began preliminary work for the 1991 Defense, and they took steps to dismiss Fay's untimely assault on the Cup. Malin

Head on, in light air, New Zealand *presented her
slimmest feature—a waterline beam of only 14 feet.*

Burnham told the *San Diego Union* that the only thing
holding up a rejection of the Kiwi Challenge was the
gathering of a complete file of America's Cup records.
And in an interview, John Marshall said this: "There is a
real sense of fair play that has to be taken into account.
A number of countries and yacht clubs are interested in
competing, and mechanisms have been worked out to
accommodate them. It is with that sense of fair play and
sportsmanship that we have to consider this challenge.
We're very concerned that what we do is absolutely fair
to every competitor."

In New Zealand, Michael Fay proudly observed the
initial construction of the biggest post-war racing sloop
ever built. At the same time, he was preparing his own
version of what was fair and right. When the document
was finished, he filed it on August 31, 1987, with the New
York Supreme Court. The very next day, he obtained a
restraining order that prevented San Diego from
announcing the date and site of the 1991 Cup. Malin
Burnham saw red, and dug in his heels for a proper

KZ-1

Designer: Bruce Farr

l.o.a.	132.8 ft.
l.w.l.	90 ft.
beam	26 ft.
w.l. beam	14 ft.
draught	21 ft.
displacement	83,000 lbs.
mast height	153.5 ft.
sail area	17,300 sq. ft.

The view from the top, looking down on the array of fifteen-foot spreaders that help support the largest carbon-fiber mast ever built for a yacht.

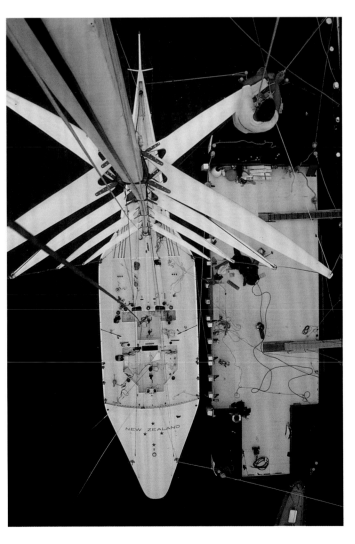

For a monohull of her size, her speed in light air is impressive.

donnybrook. New York Supreme Court Justice Carmen Beauchamp Ciparick released her decision eleven weeks later, just in time for Thanksgiving. The 19-page document reviewed San Diego's contentions that since the New Zealand boat wasn't completed it didn't constitute a "vessel"; that the Mercury Bay Boating Club Challenge would "destroy the Cup"; that the Deed of Gift should be amended to give the defender the right to designate the size of the boat; and that "literal adherence to the outmoded terms of the Deed in the face of changed circumstances would thrust the Cup into a bygone age when only those with vast wealth could compete."

In the end, Judge Ciparick's decision was brief and to the point:

". . . that Mercury Bay Boating Club has tendered a valid challenge and that San Diego Yacht Club must treat it as such in accordance with the terms of the Deed."

★

New Zealand (KZ-1), 133-feet overall, 83,000 pounds.

Ranger (J-5), 1937, 135-feet overall, 332,000 pounds.

CHALLENGE / Michael Fay: Swamp Water Fever

Fay, Richwhite & Company first started sponsoring yachting in 1983, as backers of *Southern Cross* in what was then called the Pan American Clipper Cup, an off-shore event held in Hawaii. So when Alan Bond pulled off his America's Cup coup later that year, Michael Fay was more than a casual observer of the 'round the clock hoopla going on next door.

"When Bond won the Cup we were all at the office watching the celebration on television," Fay says. "It was impressive. What a mighty and successful endeavor it was for Bond." New Zealanders were almost as excited as the Australians just for having the Cup in the same hemisphere. If there was a starting point for the colossal case of America's Cup fever Michael Fay contracted, that was probably it.

In 1984, Fay recalls reading the closing dates for entries in the 1987 America's Cup. "I nearly picked up the phone and jumped in," Fay says, "but I was very busy at the time and got distracted. So a year later, when the

On the loading dock in Auckland, New Zealand, Michael Fay poses with the mast of his Cup challenger.

opportunity to get involved arose, I was probably feeling a little guilty. Once I got started, I figured I was going down a slippery slope that I would never get back up. I recognized the swamp water fever, but I did it anyway."

New Zealand's 1987 challenge had begun with a man named Marcel Fachler, a New Zealander who was in the silver-and gold-trading business. Fachler quickly ran out of steam. Former New Zealand National Cabinet Minister Aussie Malcolm was next in. Malcolm staggered along valiantly with the project for several months until, foundering, it ended up on Fay's desk.

Fay decided there was time to make the 1987 Challenger Trials, and that there was enough sailing and design talent and available money to make it all happen. So he took charge. "The advantage I had," Fay says, "was no prior Cup knowledge. I used an analytical approach, and a lot of plain common sense. Building the two identical boats, for instance. It seemed the logical thing to do. Yet no one had ever done it."

Who is Michael Fay? During the spring of 1988 when the New Zealand entourage was arriving in San Diego, a newspaper piece about Fay quoted his step-grandfather as saying Michael was "some kind of con man." If the opposition had a good chuckle over that, so did Michael Fay. "You'd have to know my family to appreciate that remark," Fay says. "My father is retired now, but he was CEO of a group of English insurance companies. His view of life was cautious, very conservative. At the race track he might bet one dollar each way.

"My step-grandfather was a Chief Justice. He wanted me to enter the law. So I did. I graduated with the possibility of being a barrister or solicitor. But after only five months with a law firm, I left and got a job in merchant banking. The old man was disturbed. That was 1972. After a year and half I got the boot. They said I was a disruptive influence. So I opened my own office in 1974. It was about then that someone ran into my step-grandfather at his club and asked him what I was doing. He grumbled and harumphed, and told him he didn't know, he thought I was 'some kind of con man.'" Since then, the merchant banking firm of Fay, Richwhite & Company has become very large with 240 employees and offices in Auckland and Wellington, New Zealand; Sydney, Melbourne, Adelaide and Perth, Australia; London and Hong Kong; and soon, Tokyo.

Fay is a trim, boyish thirty-nine with immense energy, a bounce in his step, and the hyper-alertness of a boxer in the ring. He's got the rapid-fire delivery of a race track announcer, combined with the articulate, progressive logic of an attorney. He's quick on his feet, able to come out of the stickiest corners with a rationale so polished it brings a smile of appreciation from the listener.

As Bruce Ansley wrote in the April 2, 1988, issue of the *New Zealand Listener*, "Who is Fay like then, in the long history of the America's Cup? He is closer to the Australian raiders, the Hardys and the Bonds. But the talk in the Fay, Richwhite offices is more of the ancients, the Liptons, Sopwiths, and Vanderbilts. But despite plots on shore, they all competed on the water. Fay's real race is outmaneuvering the Americans before they get to the starting line . . . . Fay is essentially a spectator at the event itself."

Fay's initial legal stroke caught San Diegans short, and the propaganda campaign he mounted upon arriving in San Diego was in the best rowdy, Commonwealth tradition. He was receptive and good-old-boy friendly to journalists to the extent that many came away thinking they had made a pal. And the fact that he is an enthusiastic talker didn't hurt his stock with the media. His remarks have a beginning, a middle, often a quip, and usually a punch line. And he rolls on without hesitation. Ask for five minutes and you get ten.

With moral indignation, he castigated the Stars & Stripes catamarans with everything from bumper stickers to Gallup Polls aimed at generating sympathetic support for his cause. He went out and bought himself a 35-foot catamaran and (to emphasize the mismatch angle) told the press that even this little thing was whipping his big boat. That wasn't true—the boat in question was the first cat Conner had tried, and it was beaten by the 12 Meter *Liberty*—but Fay ran it up the pole anyway, as they say on Madison Avenue.

His apogee of ruthless media cleverness came just two weeks before the first Cup race. Asked to participate in a local yachting event to benefit the Cancer Society, Fay had one of his boat's 10,000 square-foot

"I'm over the top . . .

. . . and 100% fanatical . . .

. . . about the America's Cup."

gennakers imprinted with this message: "Quitting Smoking Now Greatly Reduces Serious Risks To Your Health." The sentiment would certainly please the Cancer Society. At the same time it scored a direct hit on one of Dennis Conner's major sponsors.

Fay's media campaign takes full advantage of the "mouse that roared" position: the small country verses the American giant. One reason Fay says he used the 10-month challenge option out of the Deed of Gift is that America's resources could outlast other countries over a two-or three-year haul. At a meeting in August, 1988, Fay told Sail America's Tom Ehman, "Do you realize there are more personnel, more boats, and more planes on one U.S. aircraft carrier than in the whole New Zealand military? You must try to understand this great challenge we are up against."

"The New Zealanders are overly defensive about being from a small country," Ehman says. "And we are overly defensive about criticism in the media." That combination has been a very workable platform for the launching of Fay's attacks.

Fay is highly motivated. During the New Zealand campaign in Fremantle in 1987, he told ESPN television that he wanted to bring "the America's Cup industry" to New Zealand. Of all Fay has said about the Cup, that remark continues to ring the clearest. Although Fay insists there is little payback in his Cup efforts for Fay, Richwhite & Company, his corporate identity has soared because of it. During the 1987 campaign, the performance of Capital Markets (Fay, Richwhite's listed investment company on the New Zealand Stock Exchange) could have been charted alongside the wins and losses of KZ-7. And when the New York Supreme Court ruled in favor of the challenges on November 25, 1987, Capital Market's share price rose 25 cents.

Like Lipton and Sopwith—and Bond and Hardy too—

Fay has something to sell. During the sticky negotiations with Sail America and ESPN about the placement of cameras on board New Zealand, one of the concessions Fay fought for was ownership of the television rights for Hong Kong and Tokyo.

But the Cup quest has become a lot more personal for him the more time he has put in. The 1988 campaign has been financed almost entirely by Fay, Richwhite. And with three weeks left before the 1988 races, he was assuring ESPN's Gary Jobson that if he lost, he would definitely be back for another shot at Conner.

Those who know Fay say that like Lipton and Bond, he's involved with the Cup for the long run. He's dedicated in a monastic sort of way. Fay gets up at dawn and swims before his long day There's no inter-office, after hours socializing allowed at Fay, Richwhite, and Fay's Cup camps are run in a like manner. If it sounds familiar, it should. Conner is up before dawn, walking, and similar regulations for social behavior among employees are in place at Dennis Conner Sports, Inc. The commitment of the two men co-exists on the same obsessive level: "I'm over the top and 100% ridiculously fanatical about the America's Cup," Fay has said. "I'm manic. I wake up in the middle of the night and write on pieces of paper. I ring up people all over the world and check this bit and that bit. I walk, talk, eat and breathe the bloody thing."

New Zealand writer Bruce Ainsley suggests that the folks at home feel Fay may have taken the quest a bit beyond what is fair and sporting. "We love winners, of course," Ainsley writes, "and if he cleans up in San Diego all will be forgiven. In the meantime, he tries to hold the public relations line, put the blame on the Americans, while all the time he is having a ton of fun. The America's Cup is a bloody great mud-fight! And he loves bloody great mud-fights! There's no fun if there's no wild ball. He's on a roll, it feels good." ☆

Mercury Bay, and the famous old automobile that functions as both club house and race committee headquarters for the Mercury Bay Boating Club (the horn is the starting gun). Below, M.B.B.C. Commodore Toby Morcom shepherds his flock the modern way, on two wheels.

START-UP

"We were hoping he would see that his challenge had overlooked a few things…"

On the day before Thanksgiving, 1987, Tom Ehman called the New York Supreme Court to find out if a decision was forthcoming in the matter of the New Zealand Challenge for the America's Cup. He was told that no decision was imminent. So Ehman and his wife Leslie left for a big family reunion in Michigan.

Between planes in Kansas City, Ehman called his office to wish everyone a happy Thanksgiving and check for messages. His secretary was glad he called. The office was in a tizzy. The New York Supreme Court had just ruled that Michael Fay's challenge was legitimate.

"There was one flight left that day back to San Diego," Ehman says, "but it departed from the other terminal. The place was a holiday madhouse, not a cab in sight. So I ran out and got in this cab with two ladies in the back seat. I told them I'd pay their fare if they took me to the other terminal first. They agreed. I told them it was America's Cup business. 'Oh, do you know Mr. Conner?' they asked. They said they were so proud of him. I gave them each an America's Cup pin. They wouldn't let me pay for their cab."

At 10 AM on Thanksgiving morning, there was a meeting at the San Diego Yacht Club. Included were Malin Burnham, Commodore Fred Frye, Gerry Driscoll and Harry Usher (who flew down from Los Angeles) from the America's Cup Committee, Sail America attorney Jane Ellison, and Ehman. Peter Isler, navigator aboard *Stars & Stripes 87*, represented Dennis Conner who was in Australia on business. John Marshall participated in the meeting from Maine, by speaker phone. The group worked until 3 PM, while turkeys cooled in many kitchens around San Diego.

They read Judge Ciparick's decision and considered their options. They had 30 days in which to appeal, but they decided against that. Marshall was asked to begin narrowing down the design possibilities, while Ehman would draft a letter to Fay accepting the challenge and outlining the conditions. The letter was sent to New Zealand by facsimile on December 2, 1987. Ehman wrote, "We have been guided by the terms of your notice of challenge, the Deed of Gift, and the recent ruling of the New York Supreme Court." And in fact the letter was mostly a long quote from specifics set down in the Deed. But there were a few noteworthy passages:

—"All design and construction elements, including such items as number of hulls and particulars of rigging, shall be of our choosing."

—"No other challenge will be considered until this pending event has been decided. As a corollary to this principle, the vessel of a challenger may not be substituted for your own."

—"We look forward to our success in this pending match and to staging the next America's Cup off the coast of San Diego in yachts of twelve meters, where all of the world will once again compete fairly for this trophy."

"We told Fay," Ehman says, "'Here it is, we're playing by the Deed . . . we might defend in a monohull, a multihull, a foil-assisted boat or a windsurfer.' Fay said we mentioned everything but a hot air balloon. We were hoping he would see that his challenge had overlooked a few things; that if we pressed our attack he might back off. It's like SDI (Strategic Defense Initiative). You don't get the Soviets to the table unless you start from a position of strength."

Even though they had disbanded after the victory in Perth, the Stars & Stripes braintrust that had first come together for the *Freedom* campaign in 1980 was both intact and in touch. And it was a powerful group. The 1980 campaign was so strong that Conner's trial horse, *Enterprise*, probably could have won both the defender trials and the Cup. In 1983, the weakness was design. But a measure of the deep strength of the operation was how close Conner came to winning even with a slower boat. That weakness was fixed with the "design team" approach taken in 1987, when in the end *Stars & Stripes* won going away.

"The core of the strength is in the big three," Ehman says. "Malin has a great ability to assimilate. He's a JFK-type leader. Marshall is not only a rocket scientist, he's bright, articulate, and tenacious. He's a broad-based generalist who is persuasive from the legal to the technical questions. He's a scientist with an English professor for a mother. And Dennis is a planner, a schemer. Those first days of coming to grips with the Fay challenge were our darkest moments. But Dennis said, 'I've got a plan.' Dennis always has a plan, often several plans, and one of them usually is a good one."

Tom Ehman, Executive Vice President and Chief Operating Officer of Sail America. A sailor from Lake Michigan, Ehman has been four-time North American Champion in various racing classes. In 1976 he won the USYRU Championship of Champions. Before coming to Sail America, he was Executive Director of the New York Yacht Club's America II challenge for the 1987 America's Cup. "Communications is what I'm good at. I don't carry a battle flag, nor do I have an axe to grind. My job is to get the plan out, and get people to agree to it. I grease the wheels, bring groups of people together, and open lines of communications."

John Marshall, Director of the Design Team, has been involved with the America's Cup since 1974, when he sailed with Gerry Driscoll on Intrepid. Marshall was with North Sails at the time, and was looking for 12 Meter business. He got it when the Courageous syndicate came to him for help late in the summer. Ted Hood, Courageous' sailmaker, quickly got himself on the boat. But when the Cup match of 1974 began, skipper Hood was looking unhappily at a few "North" labels as he eyed the sails. "Dennis had become starting helmsman on Courageous by then," Marshall says, "so that was the start of both Dennis' and my Cup careers." Marshall was mainsail trimmer and sailmaker for Conner in the 1980 and 1983 Cup matches.

Malin Burnham and Dennis Conner trying out a catamaran during early preparation for the 1988 America's Cup. The two former Star boat competitors sailed together on ocean racers in the 1960s and 70s. Burnham has been involved with Conner's Cup campaigns since 1980.

START-UP/Dennis Conner

Conner aboard Enterprise *preparing for the 1980 Cup campaign.*

More Than Boat Speed

One afternoon last July, Dennis Conner and crew were aboard the futuristic, 60-foot catamaran with the wing sail in the middle of San Diego Harbor. The weather was typical: the wind was light, steady and cool, the sky blue and cloudless. *Stars & Stripes (H-1)* was head-to-wind to accommodate the rubber chase boat that had come alongside. Twenty minutes earlier, while clipping along at 15 knots (in just eight knots of breeze), there had been a terrible crack when one of the boat's dagger boards had fractured just below the hull. Conner had radioed the compound, and the chase boat had delivered another one. As the broken, 12-foot board was loaded into the chase boat, Dennis Conner had an idea.

"Ask Del Cover," he said to Murph McDonnell, who was driving, "if he would cut this thing up into inch-and-a-half slices. We can mail a piece to each of our sponsors, maybe as a paper weight. Put a little brass plaque on each one saying 'Thanks for your support,' signed 'Dennis Conner.' Wouldn't that be a good idea? All these executives would

have one on their desk and their friends would ask, 'Where did you get that?' And the guy would tell them, 'Support Stars & Stripes and you'll get one too.' "

When Stars & Stripes General Manager Jerry Ladow heard this, he shook his head and chuckled. Ladow has known Conner since Dennis was a pesky kid hanging around the San Diego Yacht Club. "What you are seeing," Ladow said, "is the evolution of Dennis Conner from sailor to marketing man. Not so long ago, all he cared about was boat speed."

Dennis Conner first appeared on the America's Cup scene in 1973, when Ted Turner, the Atlanta media mogul, invited him to sail on a Cup hopeful called *Mariner*. At the time, the 29 year-old Conner was becoming known to the sailing fraternity as one of the hottest hands in the sport. He had won the Star World Championships his first year in the class (1971). He also had a Congressional Cup win under his belt—not to mention national championships in Penguins, Lightnings, and Pacific Class boats.

The quiet Conner was definitely the new kid in Newport, R.I., the

East Coast yachting bastion of blue blazers, red pants, and old money, but he wasted no time asserting himself. Pong, the first electronic television game, was popular in those days, and was played with cut-throat intensity by Turner and the Mariner crew. Conner methodically set about beating them one by one until he was undisputed house champ. And once on top, he never let anyone forget it. More salt was applied to the wounds when someone discovered that Conner had a Pong game in his home. It was revealing about the method of this hard-eyed sailor from San Diego.

With a similar application of sailing talent and management skill, Conner had progressed to the helm of *Mariner* by the end of that Cup campaign. Turner was demoted to the second boat. And when the remarkably slow *Mariner* was eliminated, Conner was invited to step aboard *Courageous* as starting helmsman and mainsheet trimmer. *Courageous* went on to win the defender trials and the Cup, having never lost a start. No freshman America's Cup sailor had ever engineered a more auspicious beginning.

At the helm of Liberty, *with navigator Halsey Herreshoff at his side, in 1983.*

Before Conner returned to the Cup scene, he spent several years sailing in the SORC, the Admirals' Cup, and other grand prix ocean-racing events. In 1976 he jumped into the 22-foot Tempest class and won an Olympic bronze medal. He began to strengthen the reputation he earned in 1973 as a man who left as little as possible to chance; whose preparation was exhaustive; and whose boats, sails, and gear were the best available. Like the Ninja warrior who stuns his opponent with the scream before the knife penetrates, Conner did everything he could to assure victory before the boats took to the water. As Cup veteran John Marshall has often said, "One of Dennis's basic rules is never to race with equal equipment if you can avoid it."

Conner's approach combined computer-like logic with text-book business management and tireless attention to detail. And when it came to the mind game, he had the sharpest needles. Other sailors began to take notice.

John Marshall entered America's Cup competition the same year as Dennis. Marshall deserted a promising career in biochemistry for sailing and sail making. He was president of North Sails for ten years before becoming CEO of the Henry R. Hinckley Company in Maine. He sailed with Conner in the 1980 and 1983 America's Cups, and was Design Team Coordinator for Dennis in 1987. Marshall recalls sailing with Conner in the 1975 Fastnet Race:

"We were on *Charisma*, owned by Jesse Philips, a high-roller from the mid-West. Dennis was a full sailing rock star by then. He had his eye on a Cup campaign, and was courting Philips. Late in the race, which was obviously lost to us, Philips wanted to employ a tactic that was inadvisable. The navigator and I argued with him about it, yet Dennis sided with Jesse, said maybe we should try it. I thought he had taken leave of his senses. Then I realized what was going on. The race was lost, so Dennis had switched to another game. That was my first encounter with Dennis the long-distance thinker."

Just five years later, Conner put together the slick 1980 campaign. After that, the Aussies came and conquered.

If Conner's loss in 1983 pulled the Cup out of its cloister at the New York Yacht Club and into world lime-light, then his comeback win in 1987 made Conner's name a household word. After the celebration was over, Conner returned to San Diego and started Dennis Conner Sports, Inc., a sports marketing company. He put up a corporate office building on the east side of the city to house D.C. Sports and his drapery business, Dennis Conner Interiors.

Conner was his own best client. He became a highly-paid ambassador to Western Australia. (In fact, when Michael Fay was in San Diego presenting his challenge, Conner was in Perth doing business.) He went on the speaking circuit at $25,000 per engagement. Product endorsements were his for the taking. This son of a San Diego fisherman began to reap the financial fruits of his sailing labors. To his previous books—*No Excuse to Lose*, with John Rousmaniere; and *Comeback*, with Bruce Stannard—Conner added a third: *The Art of Winning*, with Edward Claflin. In this book he made the transition from the race course to the fast track of business competition. Conner's philosophy had come to fruition, and he was eager to share the wealth—as long as it could be marketed. In July, prior to the New York Supreme Court's enjoinder to go race, Conner waxed philosophical during several one-hour, pre-dawn constitutionals.

I usually go to bed at 1 AM and get up a little before 5 AM. The first five minutes I don't like, but that's life. Those people still sleeping, they're the ones missing out. Is it better to be sleeping, or better to be up getting another two hours of real life drama?

Conner with Lucy and Fritz Jewett, long-time America's Cup backers, at the launching of the first of three new Stars & Stripes *in August, 1985.*

Skipper Ash Bown, with crew Jim Reynolds, Bud Caldwell, Dennis Conner, and Malin Burnham after winning the Acapulco Race in 1964.

I don't take days off and I'm never sick. Those words aren't in my vocabulary. I wouldn't know what to do with a day off. A day off, that's like being penalized. I've got to take a day off? I have to go to the penalty box? I can't score a goal that day or beat up on a rival? That's fun? That's a day off. Out of the game of life for a whole day.

Conner is a full-time, fully-focused competitor. Even after dinner and into the late hours, Conner's mind is on business, pumping out ideas. When he makes small talk, it's goal-oriented. He flies 16,000 miles a month on his American Airlines life-time pass. He's earned a black belt in the art of competition, and it shows. In *Comeback*, he wrote: "What we required of everyone was a total commitment to the commitment. I made it clear to everyone from the beginning that no one would make the team unless he or she put win-ning the Cup ahead of everything else in their lives: families, social obli-gations, money, sex, religion, friend-ships. It had to be give all or nothing at all."

Everyone is a competitor. Some show it, some are afraid to let it out. A good example is the beer can race held in the harbor every Wednesday night. It used to be for laughs. There wasn't even a start. This year all of a sudden there is a gun, a course circu-lar. Escalation. And most of the 200 boats are still out there.

The Wednesday night races are safe because no one knows you are really competing except yourself. Not even your wife. You can be a closet competitor. Only the guy inside knows. And there's someone out there with a pink jib whose been beating him regularly. So he saves $100 a month out of his wife's allowance and sneaks over to the sail maker, puts down 600 big ones and says, 'Build me a new jib.' The only condition is no bill because he doesn't want the old lady knowing. Then he goes out and whips up on Mr. Pinky. Next, Mr. Pinky visits the sail maker. Escalation.

I'm like everyone else except I stick my neck out like a snail. Some snails stick their necks out farther as they inch along. The one who keeps his neck out the longest travels the far-thest, and he's the one most exposed. If you have it out all the time, you might get a few mosquito bites, but you won't die from mos-quito bites. So I keep my neck out.

Competition is life's blood, and I'm a vampire. When I was a kid I was neighborhood champ at hide-and-go-seek. My marble bag was twice the size of anyone else's. It had to be custom made.

A competitor of Conner's agres-sive style is like an old-time fast gun. He attracts the attention of other gunslingers who have to find out if they are faster. The best of them (like Conner) will try to put the sun

and wind at their backs on the day of the showdown. Michael Fay fits the mold. He rode into town with his own deck of cards, and laid down a hand that looked bad. The initial reaction to Michael Fay's challenge was a rash of harsh invective fol-lowed by rejection. Fay bristled, and the legal war was joined. When San Diego countered with a catamaran, some sailors wondered how Conner, a monohull sailor all his life, would adjust to the multi-hull. Dennis chuckled. "Do you think a guy who won the 1977 Star Worlds with five straight firsts was worried he couldn't sail a boat with training wheels?"

Others questioned the sporting premise of the catamaran. As a way to win, it wasn't a bad tactic. Fay's surprise challenge was arguably aimed more at winning than gener-ating a memorable boat race. And winning is Conner's bottom line. But wasn't sportsmanship getting lost in the shuffle? No, says Conner.

Sportsmanship? What is sportsmanship—affording gener-osity, fairness, courtesy to your opponent? Name one top profes-sional athlete who does that. You can't because there isn't one. Sports-manship is non-existent, because professional sports—money and sports—and sportsmanship do not go hand in hand. An Australian friend of mine who plays the horses has a saying: 'Bet on self-interest—it's always running.' I'll tell you one thing, there has never been any sports-manship in the America's Cup. Any-one who thinks so is kidding himself. Check the history books.

Conner with Ted Turner in 1973 when they competed for Mariner's helm.

Our opponent Michael Fay is doing great. He's running the legal and public relations end of the Kiwi Challenge, and that's his best use. He's doing his part as a team player, and he's the star. I don't like him, but I don't dislike him either. By placing the event on hold for so long, he's made obtaining sponsors difficult for us. He screwed up our dreams for 1991. He's good, a smooth operator, a tough competitor. If not for him, who would there be to compete with? He wants a piece of the action. If people of his caliber didn't care and didn't want to make sacrifices and work so hard, it wouldn't be any fun.

Conner Watchers:

Jack Sutphen, trial horse skipper for Conner in 1983 and 1987:
" I met Dennis when I was 50. Since then, I've learned more than in the first 50 years."

John "Rambo" Grant, member of 1987 and 1988 *Stars & Stripes* crew:
"In 1987 our crew work was sloppy right to the end because Dennis was pushing so hard, challenging us with impossible situations, like last minute jibe sets. But then we were ready. He steered, and we sailed, whatever he wanted he got."

Jerry Ladow, General Manager, Stars & Stripes Syndicate:
"Dennis is at the center. The power radiates out. His life is ideas which are constantly changing. He doesn't read or write memos—there's such little stability, such little time. Like in a boat race. Everything is in his head. So his authority is personal with each person on the project. Everyone is afraid of a negative word from him. He doesn't show anger often, but everyone knows he can."

Jim Reynolds, skipper of *Betsy*, crewed for Conner on Star boats in the 1970s:
"Dennis is a risk-taker. He loves to see how close he can come to the edge."

Peter Isler, navigator on *Stars & Stripes 87* and *88*:
"Dennis loves space, time, and distance problems. On the water he constantly bets against the computer and the crew about how far and how long. In a car or even walking he's always making bets about

arrival times. He cuts things close, but his hot-dogging is aimed at learning how to maneuver in close situations."

Tom Ehman, Executive Vice President and C.O.O. of Sail America:
"Dennis is amazing. He's a good selector and motivator of people, but mainly he's a planner and a schemer. He's always got a plan—usually more than one."

Tom Whidden, main trimmer on Freedom, tactician on *Liberty* and *Stars & Stripes 87* and *88*:
"His greatest trait is his focus. Goals are dreams, but Dennis achieves them because he is smart enough to have a plan. He's good at delegating responsibility and leading by example. He wins by bludgeoning programs to death."

Michael Fay, boss of New Zealand syndicate:
"You've got to respect him as a competitor. It was impressive for him to lose, then knuckle down and go win it. I don't admire his act—sailing a catamaran against a monohull—but Conner has got to be one of the toughest guys around. He's shown amazing single-mindedness in the face of great pressure. And I must admit I have high regard for tough s.o.b.s."

☆

Conner's Racing Record

Olympics
bronze medal, Tempest class, 1976

America's Cup
1974 tactician, starting helmsman, Courageous (won, 4-0)
1980 skipper, Freedom (won, 4-0)
1983 skipper, Liberty (lost, 3-4)
1987 skipper, Stars & Stripes (won, 4-0)
1988 skipper, Stars & Stripes (won, 2-0)

World Championships
Star 1970, 1977 (Kiel, Germany; five straight firsts)

National Championships
Penguin
Lightning
PC
Star
German Match Race Champion, 1988

Congressional Cup
1973 and 1975

U.S. Admiral's Cup Team
1975, Charisma
1979, Williwaw

Onion Patch Team

Ocean Racing victories
SORC first overall four times (Stinger, Williwaw (2), Retaliation)
Acapulco Race
St. Petersburg-Ft. Lauderdale
Trans-Pacific
Mazatlan
Manzanilla
Lipton Cup
Geralia
Club de Yates Challenge Series

Maxi World Championships
1987, Emeraude

Yachtsman of the Year (four times)

San Diego Association of Yacht Clubs Yachtsman of the Year (seven times)

Conner and Marshall sailing Alex Koslov's D-Class catamaran, Invictus, *in February, 1988.*

Beat Michael Fay—In September—In San Diego

"The Court's go-ahead for the Kiwi challenge means a green light for some really far-out boats unencumbered by any rules and regulations, except the stipulation that their waterline length not exceed 90-feet . . . . The boats are going to be very big, very radical, and very controversial. The contest will not be a sailboat race. It will be a design lottery in which the sailors will have little or nothing to do with the outcome. In one word, the 1988 America's Cup challenge will be bizarre."

Dennis Conner,
from *The Bulletin* (Australia),
December 15, 1987

When news of Michael Fay's challenge was broadcast in mid-July, 1987, there were no cohesive pieces of the Stars & Stripes team left. After three very intense years, everyone had gone home to put their normal business and personal lives back together. This was especially true of the design team, most of whom had been shuttling between their offices and San Diego, Hawaii, and Fremantle during the campaign. But it wasn't long before John Marshall's telephone began ringing. "What are we going to do?" the designers wanted to know.

"I told them we were going to contest the challenge," Marshall says, "but we should start thinking. I had a lot of one-on-one conversations over the phone. We kicked the problem around."

Marshall's first premise was that the Deed of Gift doesn't provide any specification guideline other than waterline length. "There is nothing in the Deed suggesting that the challenger should write you a letter and lay down the rules. If it was adversarial, with no agreement on class of boat, then we simply had to design the fastest possible boat with a 90-foot waterline. And we had no idea about the shape of the boat Bruce Farr had designed for Michael Fay. All Fay sent was sketchy dimensions: waterline length; waterline beam; maximum beam; and draught. We didn't know if it was a trimaran, a catamaran, or a monohull. We assumed it would be a development of previous Farr boats.

"Our intuitive feeling was that a multihull would be the best," Marshall says. "Multihulls aren't very maneuverable, not great around the buoys, not teriffic in light air, but a lot of progress has been made with them. By mid-summer, a multihull was in our mind."

The design team concept first came together in 1984

for the 1987 challenge in Perth. Assembling a group of competitive designers and scientists from diverse fields to work together on a single project was an ambitious undertaking. Most of the team members had their own businesses to run, and spent many hours traveling to and from San Diego. "For 1987, we learned how to do it under those conditions," Marshall says. "We got good results. This time we had to scramble because of severe time constraints, and there was more diversity because of the unrestricted nature of the project."

Suddenly, designers who had struggled for three years to achieve small, fractional improvements in performance within the restrictive confines of the 12 Meter rule were told that a 90-foot waterline was the only limit. Marshall says that was exciting, but also frightening. "John Letcher is a fluid dynamicist who lives in Maine," Marshall says. "His interest is the science of sails, boats, and wings, and he is probably the best in the country. He was a consultant on this project. He said we were like a bunch of people who had been in prison for twenty years. Now we were on the street and we couldn't believe it. We had to find a way to deal with all the choices and options, set up a structure. So we came up with three rules that defined our parameters: we had to 1) beat Michael Fay; 2) in September; 3) in San Diego."

Several design concepts were considered for the job, including catamarans and trimarans, and Marshall was keen on a foil-assisted monohull. He discussed the possibility at length with Dr. Sam Bradfield at the University of Florida, a leading developer of the foil concept. "As a monohull, with the foils retracted in light air, the idea looked good. With the foils down for stability in moderate air, it would be very fast. And foil-borne, it would be

Conner steering Invictus. *When Fay bought this 35-footer in August, 1988, and claimed it could beat* New Zealand, *Conner knew better.* Invictus *couldn't beat* Liberty.

A
Multihull
In
Mind

The fast Formula 40 trimaran, Adrenalin, was tested by Marshall and Design Team consultant Randy Smyth when confidence in the catamaran concept was in question.

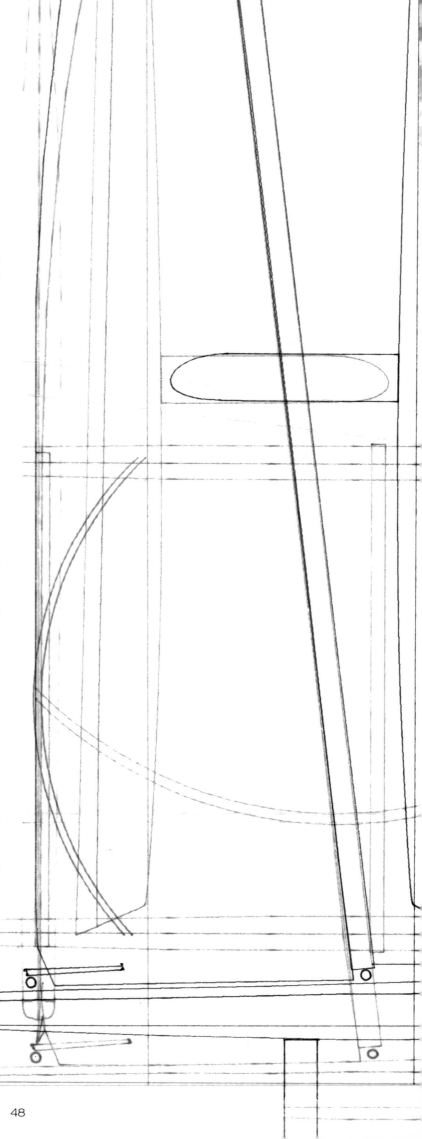

"You had to bring your boxing gloves to every meeting."

unbeatable," Marshall concluded. But designing, building and engineering such a boat would take 2 years, not the six months allotted for the project. For Marshall the scientist, who loves exploring the leading edges of every problem, abandoning the foil concept was a disappointment. "By mid-December," he says, "our thinking was centered on a catamaran."

The designers who came together with Marshall to formulate a Cup defender were Britton Chance, Dave Hubbard, Duncan MacLane, Gino Morelli, Bruce Nelson, and Bernard Nivelt. One might reasonably predict that if polarization were to occur in such a group, it would be along the monohull, multihull line. But Gino Morelli, a multihull designer, says that wasn't the case. "It was more an East Coast-West Coast division. It was jeans and sweaters vs. blue blazers. We'd meet out here, because that's where the project is. So the guys from back East would come in on the red-eye at 6 AM, having slogged through the snow to the airport. We'd show up rested, enjoying the great weather."

Marshall says the design team discussions had a Quaker Meeting atmosphere. "Nothing ever came to a vote, but we did talk problems to death." Gino Morelli paints a more robust picture: "A lot of decisions were made based on who could talk the longest and loudest. You had to bring your boxing gloves to every meeting."

Once the catamaran concensus had been arrived at, size was the next issue. The proposals ranged from a 44-foot boat that would be small, quick, clean, and fast to build, all the way to a 90-footer. "In the end," Marshall says, "we opted for a boat that would be in the water on schedule so we could have plenty of time for practice, and that would present a minimum of breakdowns. I have the feeling now that we could have gone to 75 feet. But I'm happy. I see boats that will get the job done. They're lighter, they require a smaller crew. We'll accomplish more with less."

Next was the rig. Dave Hubbard and Duncan MacLane had been brought onto the design team because of their long involvement with the Little America's Cup, an international event sailed in 25-foot C-Class catamarans. Since

Britton Chance, Jr.

Britton Chance, Jr.'s involvement with the America's Cup began in 1962 when he worked on the design for Nefertiti with Ted Hood. In 1969, he drew Chanceggar for Baron Marcel Bich as a trial horse for the French campaign. In 1970, he modified Intrepid, which beat Gretel II for its second straight Cup victory. In 1974, he designed Mariner.

In 1987, Chance joined the Stars & Stripes design team. His experience with multihulls goes back to 1963 when Jack Potter, for whom Chance had designed Equation, commissioned him to design a 40 foot trimaran. The boat, Touché, was advanced for its day. It featured equal volume floats, a fully battened sail, and a rotating mast. Construction was foam sandwich, with the use of epoxy resins.

The first boats Chance designed were 5.5 Meters, the glamour boat of the early 60s. His best-known design is probably Equation, a slender 65-foot ocean racer later renamed Inverness. Other notable designs by Chance: Ondine (an 80-footer, 1973); Resolute Salmon (One Ton); Bay Bea (1977 Admiral's Cup team); and Wildflower (Two Ton). Brit is President of Chance & Co., Naval Architects, in Essex, Connecticut.

David Hubbard

Dave Hubbard was born in Belfast, Northern Ireland, and grew up in Essex, Devonshire, England. He moved to Connecticut in 1949, and graduated from MIT in 1951. He currently is employed as an engineer with the Pitney Bowes Company in Norwalk, Ct.

Hubbard built and sailed dinghies as a boy, and built a 16-foot catamaran in the early 50s after moving to the U.S. From that point on, he was active in racing both multi- and mono-hulls. In the 1960s, he began sailing and designing C-Class catamarans. In 1968, the first C-Class wing sail was attempted by the Danes. Hubbard joined Tony Di Mauro's Patient Lady Little America's Cup campaign in 1970, and designed the first successful wing sail in 1971. It rested on a turntable ten feet across that rotated 360 degrees. In 1973, Hubbard designed a wing sail with two elements, or "flaps," that was the ancestor of the wing used by Stars & Stripes '88.

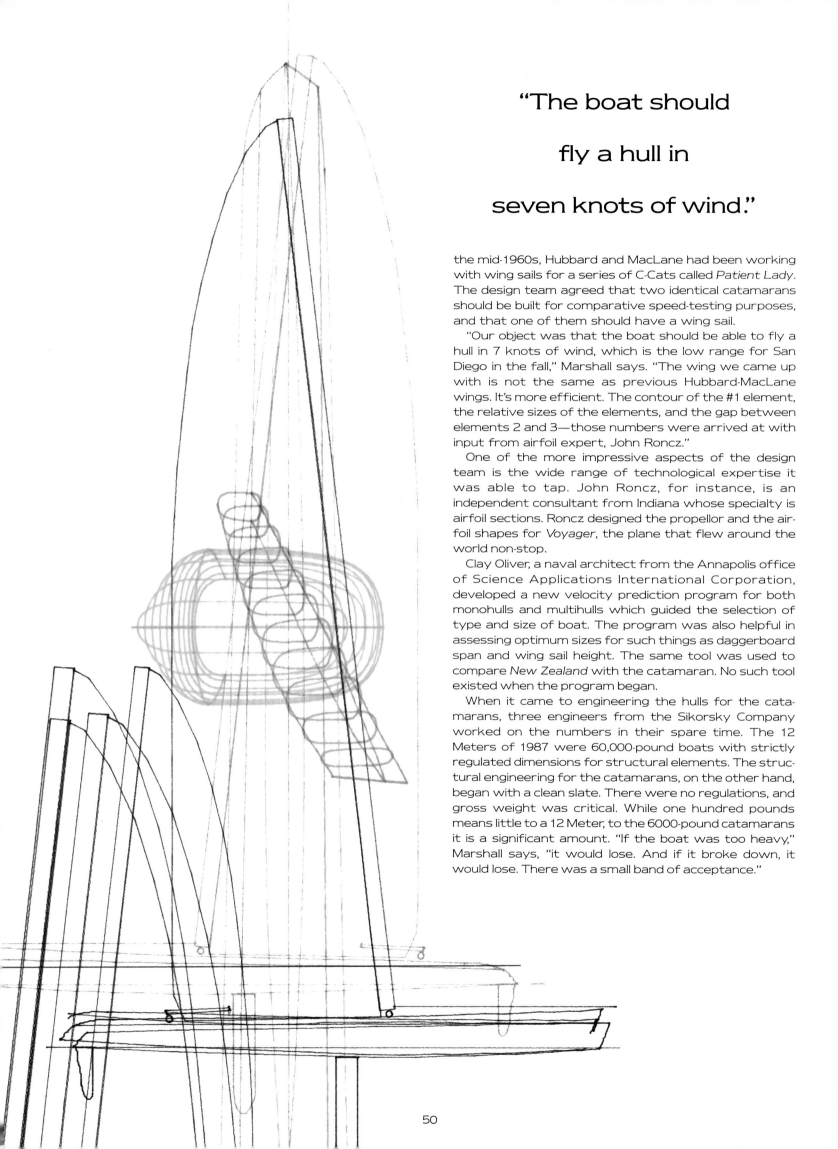

"The boat should fly a hull in seven knots of wind."

the mid-1960s, Hubbard and MacLane had been working with wing sails for a series of C-Cats called *Patient Lady*. The design team agreed that two identical catamarans should be built for comparative speed-testing purposes, and that one of them should have a wing sail.

"Our object was that the boat should be able to fly a hull in 7 knots of wind, which is the low range for San Diego in the fall," Marshall says. "The wing we came up with is not the same as previous Hubbard-MacLane wings. It's more efficient. The contour of the #1 element, the relative sizes of the elements, and the gap between elements 2 and 3—those numbers were arrived at with input from airfoil expert, John Roncz."

One of the more impressive aspects of the design team is the wide range of technological expertise it was able to tap. John Roncz, for instance, is an independent consultant from Indiana whose specialty is airfoil sections. Roncz designed the propellor and the air-foil shapes for *Voyager*, the plane that flew around the world non-stop.

Clay Oliver, a naval architect from the Annapolis office of Science Applications International Corporation, developed a new velocity prediction program for both monohulls and multihulls which guided the selection of type and size of boat. The program was also helpful in assessing optimum sizes for such things as daggerboard span and wing sail height. The same tool was used to compare *New Zealand* with the catamaran. No such tool existed when the program began.

When it came to engineering the hulls for the cata-marans, three engineers from the Sikorsky Company worked on the numbers in their spare time. The 12 Meters of 1987 were 60,000-pound boats with strictly regulated dimensions for structural elements. The struc-tural engineering for the catamarans, on the other hand, began with a clean slate. There were no regulations, and gross weight was critical. While one hundred pounds means little to a 12 Meter, to the 6000-pound catamarans it is a significant amount. "If the boat was too heavy," Marshall says, "it would lose. And if it broke down, it would lose. There was a small band of acceptance."

Duncan MacLane

In the 1950s and 60s, Duncan MacLane's father was manufacturing a catamaran called an Aqua Cat in Norwalk, Ct. A local fellow named Tony Di Mauro was an Aqua Cat dealer. A fleet of the small cats blossomed at Roton Point, with Duncan MacLane in the forefront. He won the class National Championship four years in a row. When Tony Di Mauro began his Patient Lady campaigns for the Little America's Cup in the late 60s, MacLane was his helmsman of choice.

MacLane won the Little America's Cup in 1977, 1978, 1980, and 1982 before losing to the Australians in 1985. MacLane's Patient Lady experience led him into naval architecture. After graduating from Webb Institute, where his thesis advisor was the hydrofoil expert Sam Bradford, MacLane took a job in Wilton, Ct., with a tug boat designer named Clancy Horton. When Horton passed away a few years ago, Duncan took over Horton and MacLane. When he isn't thinking about wing sails and airfoil shapes, MacLane can be found designing tug boats.

Gino Morelli lived in Texas until he was 13. His father designed, built, and drove modified drag racers. Gino grew up in the pits. He says if he hadn't moved to California, he'd be racing cars.

In California, the Morellis acquired a 24-foot sailboat and taught themselves how it worked. Soon they wanted something bigger and faster. Gino and his father built a 34-footer (that's what would fit in the back yard), a trimaran for speed. "It took me ten years to figure out that in this culture, there's something wrong with multihulls," Gino says with a laugh.

He began building catamarans in every spare moment, and after a stint at Hobie, began to dominate the 18-square-meter business. Since then he has designed and built cats of all sizes, become a force in the Formula 40 class, and survived a full cartwheel at 28 knots in a 65-foot catamaran while racing in the Mediterranean.

Gino Morelli

A final flurry
of anxiety: would it
be fast enough?

There were several design team meetings during the month of December. At the same time, John Marshall and Dennis Conner went sailing on a number of different multihulls just to get the feel, and to do on-board evaluation of the various theories being expressed. By January 1, the design team was certain of the concept. It had taken four weeks to define the boat numerically. By February 1, all detailing, structural engineering, and lines had been finished, and the design was fixed. "It had gotten a bit bigger, attained its 60-foot length," Marshall says. "Then we suffered a final flurry of anxiety. Was it fast enough? We thought so. We had two good rigs. But the idea of this 60-footer going up against a 120-foot monster filled us with paranoia. Would we get destroyed? We didn't think so. We had more intelligence on the New Zealand boat by this time.

"We had gotten very good at taking two 12 Meters and predicting their performance down to one second per mile on the computer. With the catamarans, we were off by probably a minute a mile. And no computer in the world will tell you how much a catamaran will be slowed down in rough water. As sailors, we knew it would happen, but we couldn't quantify it."

Nervous, Marshall began thinking about adding a third boat. He and design team member Randy Smythe had sailed a trimaran called *Adrenalin* in Florida, and had been impressed. And Bernard Nivelt had been pushing for a trimaran since design team meetings began. Maybe a 75-foot version of *Adrenalin* was the answer. Marshall: "But if we added a third boat, a tri, what would happen to time, money, and human resources? We debated. The race was on a certain day, and we had to be there. On the other hand, more time in court was ahead: maybe there wouldn't even be a race. Money was uncertain. Dennis was working on sponsors who were understandably reluctant because of the event's uncertainty. We had to be cost-effective. And we had such good sailors, such a dedicated crew. They had limits. There was only so much we could do in the allotted time. So we took a deep breath and went ahead with the two cats."

Computer sketches courtesy of Gino Morelli

Bernard Nivelt moved permanently to the United states following the success of his design, Diva, which was top boat in the 1983 Admiral's Cup and winner of the 1984 S.O.R.C. His U.S. office, Joubert Nivelt Designs, is in Mystic, Connecticut.

Joubert Nivelt is one of the few design firms that has done equally well with both monohulls and multihulls. Their 75-foot catamaran Charentes Maritime has several big wins to her credit, including the La Rochelle-New Orleans Race. And Fleury-Michon, an 85-foot cat, won the Route de la Decouverte race.

Sprint, a Joubert Nivelt One-Tonner, was named Boat of the Year in 1984 and 1986. Also in 1986, the One-Tonner Silverstar took first in class and first overall in the Bermuda Race. Another Joubert Nivelt design, Abracadara (a 43-footer), won the S.O.R.C., and was first in class, third overall to Bermuda.

Nivelt is currently working on a Whitbread maxi, UBS Finland, and several monohulls for the next B.O.C. single-handed race. Cruising catamarans are also on the drawing boards at Joubert Nivelt.

Bernard Nivelt

Bruce Nelson

Bruce Nelson received his degree from the University of Michigan School of Naval Architecture, where he was a three-time All-American sailor. One of his first successful boats was the Quarter-Tonner Blivit, which was North American champion in 1978.

With Bruce Marek, Nelson began Nelson/Marek Yacht Design, Inc., in 1978. Rush, built to the old One-Ton rating, brought the firm national recognition by winning the One-Ton North Americans in 1980. Their Stars & Stripes, a 39-foot ocean racer, was the top U.S. boat on the Admiral's Cup team in 1981.

Since 1983, Nelson/Marek has produced a number of successful ultra-light-displacement "maxi sleds" in the 68-foot range. In the 1985 Trans-Pac Race, Nelson/Marek boats finished one-two-three, and took the first three places in Class A. In 1987, Drumbeat was first in Class A and first overall.

In 1988, the Nelson-designed Challenge 88 won the Canada One-Ton Cup.

Nelson was a member of the 1987 as well as the 1988 Stars & Stripes design team. His employees include 1987 Stars & Stripes bow man Scott Vogel.

START-UP/Conner Camp
Shaking The Tree

T om Ehman recalls sitting in Malin Burnham's kitchen one evening in December, 1987, with Malin and Dennis Conner. "It was a difficult time. We had no money. We didn't know what kind of boat Fay was building, but we knew we couldn't go for a run-of-the-mill boat. We thought we could do a catamaran under the Deed. Dennis said he was looking at a no-win scenario. If he won in a cat, people would shrug. If he lost, it would be a disaster. Malin said he had to do it. Dennis said he hadn't even had a chance to savor the win in Australia. Malin said that was true for all of us. Dennis was quiet a minute. 'Then I guess I'll have to do it,' he said."

Dennis Conner faces the press.

Modern America's Cup competition probably presents a broader range of challenges than any other sport. That's why most Cup syndicates have bureaucratic divisions of labor and responsibility akin to any twenty million-dollar business. At the head of most syndicates is a managing board of directors which has the power to make all decisions.

Stars & Stripes has such a organization. And The Sail America Foundation, which began life as a syndicate, and which is now charged with conducting the defense and running the regatta, is a veritable maze of bureaucratic tendrils. But the difference in the San Diego America's Cup scene is Dennis Conner. When he was in Newport, R.I., in 1973, Conner had a great opportunity to study the workings of two syndicates. One, the Mariner group, was the MacHale's Navy of syndicates: it was great fun, but not very productive. The other, the Courageous group, was good enough to win. But both were fraught with disagreement, politics, personality clashes, and job uncertainty. In those days, Cup skippers were fired with depressing regularity.

So when Conner made his move to defend the Cup in 1980, it was with one basic condition: he would be in charge overall, with a no-cut contract. He also wanted two boats. He got what he wanted, made it stick, and with a landslide victory proved he was on the right track. Since then, Conner has remained in charge. He is the only modern Cup skipper ever to command so much power.

Any Cup campaign can be broken down into ten specialized areas, any one of which could be a full-time career. And as Michael Fay says, "You must get an A in each of them to win." They are: Fund Raising; Design and Technology; Sailing and Tactics; Sails; Personnel Recruitment and Management; Logistics; Marketing; Media Relations; Legal; and Sponsor Fulfillment. With the exception of Design, Logistics, and Legal—which he keeps close track of—Dennis Conner personally is in charge of the other seven.

Conner began to learn the craft of fund raising in 1973, when he made his first contacts in Newport. After *Enterprise* lost in 1977, Conner was recruited by that syndicate. The

result was the *Freedom* campaign of 1980, a big win which improved his stock and his connections. Conner applied himself to fund raising. As one Conner loyalist puts it, "He's good at shaking the tree."

Potential sponsors always want to meet the skipper. Conner has always been happy to oblige. He's also good at making the deals. After his momentous loss in 1983, Conner picked himself off the deck, and with patriotism on his side, began the Dennis Conner Crusade to retrieve the Cup. He committed, the sponsors believed, and he delivered. After he won in 1987, his corporate access became phenomenal.

Fund raising for the 1991 defense began immediately after *Stars & Stripes* crossed the line in the last race of 1987. "Fund raising is on-going," Conner says. "At first I was raising money for myself to mount a defense for the next time. I started with the people who had helped us in 1987 and had a product to sell."

Conner had recruited Pepsi, Philip Morris, Merrill-Lynch, and Ford to sponsor *Stars & Stripes* in the 12 Meter World Championships in Sardinia in 1987. Conner bought time on ABC TV and produced two one-hour shows that were well-received. When the Fay challenge arrived and the financial need became critical, Conner had the rapport he needed to call again. A measure of the confidence those corporations had in Conner was reflected by his rate of success: three out of four said yes.

"The unsung heros of America's Cup XXVII are the sponsors," Conner says. "Mike Lorelli at Pepsi committed first, giving us that important initial foundation block. Then Bill Campbell at Marlboro joined us. Then Dan Tully and Bill Schreyer at Merrill-Lynch. They all took a chance. Despite the climate on Wall Street at the time, Merrill-Lynch decided to help defend our country's pride and honor. It's easy to give in the good times. They stepped up when it wasn't easy. It took a lot of foresight and commitment to the Cup.

When it comes to sailing and tactics, Conner's record speaks for itself. But equally important is the less obvious side, the design and execution of the sailing program that brings boats and crews up to full potential. The thoroughness of Conner's sail-testing programs is legendary. They're quality programs as well. "Dennis knows when we're off

track," Tom Whidden says. "And when we have a bad set-back with the program—when something breaks that will take days to repair—he knows how to spend the time in a worthwhile fashion. When funds are limited, he knows the best way to spend the money."

Conner avoided the media in the early years. He didn't have the magnetism of a Ted Turner, or the glib tongue of a Tom Blackaller. He isn't a natural talker, and cameras made him nervous. But when he realized this part of the game was becoming important, he studied it. He's become adept at the tactics of the media game. His media-demand rating is high, and he now gives a good interview. Mainly he's learned to project his unique personality. What you see is what you get, and as usual, that's a workable approach for dealing with the media.

Marketing is a skill Conner learned as a young carpet salesman, and he's gotten better at it through the years. When it comes to marketing both himself and the America's Cup, Conner rarely lets an opportunity pass untested.

Many world class sailors end up making sails because they've spent a lifetime trimming them. Conner is not a sailmaker, but he could be. "He's my best customer, and my toughest because he is so demanding," Tom Whidden says. "He can drive me crazy. Next to me, he knows best how to recut a sail."

One reason Conner has such success with sponsors is his insistence on fulfilling his end of deals. He does it almost to a fault, if that's possible in the sponsorship game. But those in the maddening business of prodding athletes forgetful of reaching for the sponsor's colors at the moment of victory watch Conner's performance with appreciation.

Among the numerous friends and dignitaries Conner took sailing on the catamaran was ten year-old Molly O'Bryan.

What Conner is most proud of on this amazing scorecard is the people he has recruited over the years, and whom have stayed with his program. It is not easy to work for Dennis Conner. He leads by example, and no one quite matches the intensity of his daily routine. For those who think their reach should exceed their grasp, the standard is established. And from the looks, there are plenty who are enthusiastic about putting their commitment to winning the Cup ahead of everything else in their lives; ahead of "families, social obligations, money, sex, religion, friendships," as Conner has written.

"Dennis is good at the selection of people and the delegating of responsibility," says Tom Whidden, who may know Dennis best. "He's smart enough to know this is a team sport. Many skippers try to be a sole nucleus. Dennis makes nuclei out of a lot of different people."

As America's Cup XXVII got off to its shaky start, there was some grumbling from other potential defenders who felt they had been closed out of the Fay challenge. But it was clear that only one American syndicate had the people, the resources, and the ability to mobilize in time to meet this challenge. That was Stars & Stripes. ★

Having fun with John Horgan, Chairman of the Western Australian Development Corporation, for whom Conner is an ambassador.

Political Footballs

Doing what he does best: Michael Fay holding court with the media.

The perilous path to America's Cup XXVII proved that a challenge presented without mutual consent is like crashing the formal ball wearing motorcycle boots and a gun. It does nothing but start trouble.

By the time Michael Fay's challenge had been declared legal in court, the world 12 Meter corps had rallied.

Fay with attorneys George Tomkins and Andrew Johns.

Twenty-two syndicates from ten nations had submitted earnest money along with letters of intention to participate in America's Cup XXVII. Tom Ehman's letter of December 2, 1987, delivered the disturbing news of their exclusion. The Fay challenge would be treated by the letter of the Deed of Gift—one-on-one. That decision did not win friends in the America's Cup world. The issue of a challenger series became a political football, Aussie rules variety. It took a number of odd bounces that were difficult to follow.

On December 10, there was a meeting in New York between Alan Bond, Peter deSavary, Michael Fay, Malin Burnham, and six other America's Cup groups. Pressure was brought to bear for a multi-national challenger series in boats of 90-foot waterline. Fay agreed. Sail America did not. Fay would continually use this to his advantage in the media, telling all who would listen that Sail America was the villain who shut out the world. Alan Bond would agree with his neighbor from Down Under. But that was only half the tale.

In the spring of 1988, after a winter-long series of law suits and proposals submitted by Britain's Peter deSavary on behalf of his Blue Arrow syndicate, Fay himself closed the door when it became evident that Blue Arrow's foil-assisted boat was anything but the specific 90-foot monohull Fay was insisting upon. And when Iain Murray came forward through the Cruising Yacht Club

Design Team Director John Marshall advised a catamaran defender and a race in Long Beach where the winds are reliably stronger in September. When the big cat's excellent light air capability became apparent, the site was switched back to San Diego.

of New South Wales with a 90-footer far removed from *New Zealand*'s general description, Fay once again shook his head. Sail America had by then agreed to both the Blue Arrow and Cruising Yacht Club entries. Fay's change of mind would not help his case in court.

In January, 1988, three days of discussions among Michael Fay and representatives from Sail America, the America's Cup Defense Committee, and the San Diego Yacht Club were held in San Diego. A compromise plan was on the table that called for the Cup to be held in boats of 70-foot waterline in San Diego in 1990. The plan included a multi-national challenger round. Whether or not Michael Fay was seriously considering this plan is a matter of conjecture. But discussions were brought to an abrupt end when Sail America announced it would defend in a multihull. Fay's campaign against the catamaran began immediately, as did his intention to challenge the legality of such a defender in court.

The site of the races became an issue once again in February, 1988, ·when Sail America and the San Diego Yacht Club announced that Long Beach had been selected. This was puzzling to many Cup observers, who couldn't fathom how the San Diego Yacht Club, having been bloodied by their fervent efforts to keep the races in the city, had agreed to let Long Beach steal the scene. But at the time, there was good reason.

Early results from the Velocity Prediction Program indicated that the 60-foot catamaran would be vulnerable in light air. San Diego's average winds for September were 6 to 9 knots. Long Beach's average was 9 to 11 knots. "It doesn't sound like a big difference," John Marshall says, "but it is. Once you do the computations for wind energy, Long Beach was better by a factor of 2.75." So Marshall went to the Yacht Club Board and outlined the situation. If the race was held in San Diego, there was a chance the cat would be beaten. Reluctantly, the Board voted to move the event to Long Beach. An official announcement to that effect was made on February 5.

Just a month later, with new numbers in hand, Marshall again appeared before the Yacht Club Board. "We felt confident at that time that we had substantially more potential in the lighter ranges. And on the other side, we

Gerry Driscoll, Chairman of the America's Cup Committee, was unhappy about the decision to defend in a multihull. He suggested building a monohull as well. "Why not take the Kiwis on in a 90-foot monohull if that's what the tool is?" Driscoll asked. He tried to short-cut what he saw as a "personal vendetta" between Burnham and Fay by negotiating directly with Fay. Driscoll even held his own press conference at one point. "I argued as hard as I could," Driscoll says, "but I couldn't get anywhere." Driscoll worries about the growing commercialism of the Cup: "Wimbledon has a certain grace about it that doesn't distract. Indianapolis, on the other hand, is a carnival. Right now the Cup is a carnival. It needs more quality and grace."

Jerry LaDow, General Manager of Stars & Stripes. "The problem with this event is that it hasn't matured," LaDow says. "Professional golf and other sports have structured rules. This is like the Persian Market Place."

John "Rambo" Grant was a grinder on the Stars & Stripes team in 1987. He was working for Dennis Conner Sports, Inc., when he got the call to take charge of building the compound. Rambo, an ex-Marine, was equal to the task.

were under assault from Fay. Sail America, the Yacht Club, Stars & Stripes, and the community needed to present a united front. Fay was antagonistic, skilled at public relations. Why give him an easy target? And San Diego wanted to host the event. I told the Board we would be competitive here. The Board quickly voted to bring the Cup back to San Diego."

With the design of the defender settled, the site selected, and construction underway, the building of the Stars & Stripes compound on 8th Avenue began. Like everything else, it was a hurry-up situation. John "Rambo" Grant, a member of the 1987 *Stars & Stripes* crew, was assigned to plan and build the facility.

As much as anything else in the Stars & Stripes campaign, the compound reflected the ingenuity, ability, and can-do spirit of the team. A handful of hard working sailors turned a grease-stained dirt-patch of R.E. Staite Engineering, Inc. (a marine contractor), into one of the finest yacht yards in San Diego, maybe the West Coast. And they did it with the speed of a circus crew erecting the big top. "We had it planned out," Rambo says, "but we couldn't begin moving stuff in until May 16. The boats rolled in from the builder on May 19. Then the wing arrived. Everything was in pieces. We had to assemble everything, paint the boat, finish driving piles, move in the crane, and have everything in place for an official unveiling on May 25th."

By August, when the sponsors and the press arrived in force and it was time to go public, the compound was not only meticulously organized and efficient, it even had a pretty face complete with awnings, steps, handsome tables, and a public viewing window. And free Pepsi Cola and Klondike bars!

Both in the yard and the office, the staff labored around the clock. Jerry LaDow, a long-time friend of Conner, was general manager of the operation. "It was an intense, confused program," LaDow said. "With 12 Meters, we at least knew what we were building. With the catamarans, only a few guys knew. Would they be built right? We had no experience with the builders, R.D. Boat Works. We were all strangers thrown into the mix. But it all got done on time. The wing worked out of the box. The boat was right. The suppliers and subcontractors delivered."

But LaDow noted a large difference from past Cup campaigns. "This year it was cash and carry, nothing on credit. Too many people had to wait too long after the last Cup. The line about helping win the Cup for mother, God, and country didn't work any more. Suppliers wanted a substantial deposit up front, and the balance on time. This year we got away from the good ol' boy approach and into professionalism."

The Stars & Stripes compound at its prime, with both catamarans rigged and in residence. The wing boat sits on its hydraulic tilt mechanism. The first, smaller wing functions as an awning above the electronics and paint shops on container row. The flat roof (top, middle) is the administration building. The tender, Betsy (far left), is docked next to the Chart House restaurant. Chase boats and sails in blue bags are along the floating dock beneath the flag. The tent (far right) covers the metal and woodworking shops, and the sailmaker's repair shop. Although the cats weigh only three tons, the crane is capable of lifting 90 tons.

START-UP / Old Home Week

Winning America's Cup efforts are powered by the right people pulling together in the right way. One reason Stars & Stripes was in position to respond to an emergency defense of the Cup was the core crew of loyalists which had been honed to a fine competitive edge by the long months of training and commitment in Hawaii and Western Australia. When word of Michael Fay's challenge got out, many of these people called and asked what they could do. The answer: plenty. Soon, it was old home week in San Diego as the Stars & Stripes clan gathered after only a 10-month respite. As Conner said with obvious pride in his troops, "Most of them were my guys from last time. I blew the whistle, and here they came." ☆

Conner with Maria Flannigan, his assistant at D.C. Sports. Maria spent much of her time at the compound as the Cup pace quickened.

Kerry Geraghty, yard manager, wearing radio headset while working with the crane operator. From 1978 to 1987, Geraghty owned and operated a custom race-boat yard. During that time he built 48 ocean racers. Born in Los Angeles, Kerry moved to San Diego 15 years ago. Why? "Better golf courses."

"J.B.," John Barnitt, sailor. John was on the S&S 87 team, then went to work for D.C. Sports. He began the 1988 campaign working on the Formula 40s, then joined the compound builders. A sailing team member, John's official title is "Dr. Whack 'n' Hack."

At the controls of the compound's 90-ton crane, Donn Wuest was travel lift driver and welder through the S&S 87 campaign in Hawaii and Fremantle. For 1988 he was given the tricky responsibility of launching the catamarans.

A 1978 graduate of the New York Maritime College, Bill Trenkle met Conner through the Ft. Schuyler Foundation. In 1980 he drove a chase boat, then sailed on Freedom and Enterprise. He helped build all the boats for the 1983 campaign, and sailed on the trial horse. In 1987 he recommissioned the boats, trained the crew, and was a tailer on S&S 87. Trenkle joined D.C. Sports in 1987. He was Stars & Stripes operations manager in 1988, and jib trimmer on the sailing team.

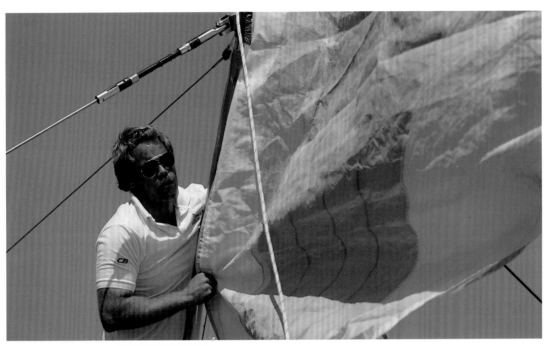

Tom Whidden has been sailing with Conner since 1978, when Conner asked him to drive the trial horse. Tailer on Freedom in 1980, he was Conner's tactician aboard Liberty in 1983, and Stars & Stripes 87 and 88. Whidden is President of North Sails, Inc.

An All-American sailor from Yale, Peter Isler became navigator on Stars & Stripes 87 after a short stint as skipper of Courageous. World match racing champion in 1986, Isler joined D.C. Sports in 1987. He was navigator on S&S 88.

Fritz and Lucy Jewett backed Courageous in 1974, and Enterprise in 1977. Since 1980, they have been solidly behind Dennis Conner's campaigns.

Barbara Schwartz (left), was assistant to Lesleigh Green (center), head of S&S public relations. An Australian, Lesleigh worked for Alan Bond in 1983, joined Conner in 1987. LaMonta McLarty (right) is a Texan living in Australia who was recruited by Conner in 1987. Assistant to Jerry LaDow, LaMonta is known as the Red Adair of office management.

John Engle (middle) has been with Sail America Foundation since 1986. He joined Stars & Stripes in 1988 to coordinate sponsor relations at the compound.

Jim Reynolds has been ocean racing with Conner since the 1960s. He crewed for Dennis in 1971 when they won the Star World Championships. In 1988, Reynolds was chase boat driver.

Former sailmaker and long-time 12 Meter sailor Jack Sutphen was replaced by Conner on Courageous in 1974. He later joined the 1980 Freedom campaign as trial horse driver, and has been with Conner ever since. The elaborate diaries of boat performance Sutphen writes religiously are invaluable.

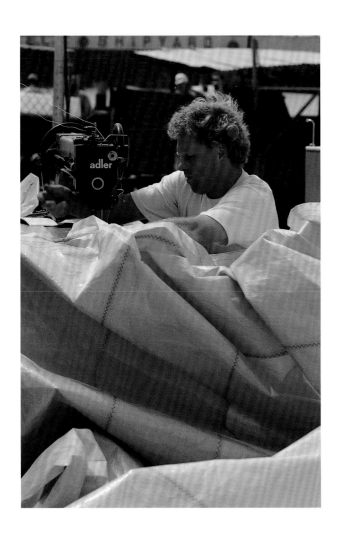

Lars Linger (left), who worked for North Sails in New Zealand and San Francisco, was on the Stars & Stripes sailmaking team. Del Cover, (above), is a furniture maker who can build anything—and did.

Steve Avedesian was tender driver for Buddy Melges' Heart of America campaign in 1987. Afterwards, he worked with Conner in 1987 at the 12 Meter World Championships in Sardinia. He was asked to drive the tender, Betsy, in 1988.

Australian M.S. "Red" Webb was hired Down Under in 1987 as bodyguard for Conner after his life was threatened. Red came to San Diego to be chief of compound security for the 1988 defense.

Linda Schneider (with daughter Lindsey), worked as compound receptionist while husband Mike (below) chased cats. Mike is an underwater specialist whose talents came in handy when the modified Formula 40 catamarans began capsizing. The Schneiders live on a 1946 Henry Nevins 10 Meter at the San Diego Yacht Club.

Pierre LeMaout is a top professional Formula 40 sailor from France who was recruited by Conner to be trial helmsman.

Catamaran expert John Wake has worked with Hobie Alter (research and development), and R.D. Boat Works, builder of the big cats. Wake was in charge of both catamaran's hulls.

Skip Banks has won the Little America's Cup four times (with Duncan MacLane). He was with Tony DiMauro's Patient Lady campaign for 17 years. Banks was on the S&S 88 sailing team as wing-camber trimmer.

Murray "Murph" McDonnell is a New Zealander who used to work for Kerry Geraghty. In 1987, he and Kerry sawed off the keel winglets of S&S 87 and built new ones in time for the final challenger trials. Murph was on the 1988 compound crew.

"Wing Nuts" in flight. Left to right: Pieter Denhartog, wing builder; Duncan MacLane and Dave Hubbard, wing designers; Dana Timmer, wing foreman/builder; Terry Richards, wing builder; and Skip Banks, who has been handling wing-powered cats for 15 years.

Dana Timmer, applying clear 3 M heat-shrink plastic film to the wing sail. Timmer commuted to the Mojave Desert wing-fabricating plant in the 175 mph Rutan Long-eze aircraft he built.

Mickey Munoz dressed for depositing good-luck garlic inside the bow of US-1. Former big wave surfer and movie double, Munoz is a former R.D. boat builder who joined the compound crew.

Dory Vogel, the only woman ever to sail aboard a 12 Meter in an America's Cup trial race (1987), was back in 1988 to assist the electronics and technical team in the spy program.

Boston resident Cam Lewis, twice winner of the Finn Gold Cup and a regular aboard large, ocean catamarans, worked with Carl Buchan trimming the wing-sail on Stars & Stripes 88.

Randy Smyth, who won a Olympic Silver Medal in the Tornado catamaran in 1984, brought practical sailing considerations to design team meetings, and considerable multihull expertise to the crew of S&S 88. Randy runs Sails by Smyth in Newport Beach, Ca.

Carl Buchan, who won an Olympic Gold Medal in 1984 (crew, Flying Dutchman), was at the top of Conner's list of draftees for the sailing team. Buchan was wing-sail trimmer on Stars & Stripes.

TESTING

The snub-nosed Formula 40 (above and opposite), turbo-charged Stars & Stripes version; not for the faint of heart.

Formula Dangerous

Modified Formula 40. It sounds like an outsized race car, or the latest in renegade Outback rebel vehicles from a *Road Warrior* sequel. It's not. The Formula 40 is a multihull race boat, probably the fastest class boat of its size in the world. It was developed as an alternative to the maxi catamarans that were getting out of financial range, even for sailing-mad European sponsors. The Formula 40 Class concept was born in Europe, where a well-organized circuit now exists. And it is the boat of choice for the U.S. Pro Sail tour. Formula 40s are exciting to watch, exhilarating to sail as they reach speeds of 20 knots and more. Approached with care and concentration they are manageable. Soup them up and the story is different.

Formula 40s were Stars & Stripes' answer to the problem of crew training. With the 60-foot cats under construction, there was nothing even vaguely similar in the San Diego area for the crew to sail. So in early March, two used 40s were purchased in France and air freighted to the U.S. in pieces. Two weeks later the crew was sailing the boats in San Diego Harbor.

When one of the 40s broke a mast on a particularly windy day, the consensus was to rebuild it taller. The other 40 lost a mast, and it too got a bigger stick. "Dennis would ask, 'Why did it break?' and we would figure that out," Peter Isler says. "Then he would ask, 'Can we make it bigger?' And we would. Dennis was in his element this time because there were no rules. He

kept piling sail area on the 40s, and on the 60s when they arrived. 'Sail area is king,' was Dennis' slogan."

The first modification simply added ten feet to each of the 63-foot masts, increasing sail area from 967 to 1197 square feet. "People felt that wasn't scary enough," Duncan MacLane says, although one of the boats suffered a spectacular dismasting after that alteration. On a screaming reach in 18 knots true wind, the baby stay broke and the mast collapsed like a wet noodle. Two weeks later, the other mast went down after the compression failure of a spreader.

Modification #2 bumped the mast up another eight feet, with sail area increasing to 1350 square feet. Also, the cross beams were cut from 23 feet to 16 feet, a substantial reduction in both beam and stability. Now the two Formula 40s were very mean broncos. They were renamed "DC 40s."

The theory was to modify the boats so they would behave more like the 60-footers, with lots of horsepower for the light San Diego winds. That way, Conner and crew could become accustomed to the projected feel of the bigger boats. The 40s, as delivered, would fly a hull in 12 knots of breeze. The 60-footers were designed to fly a hull in six to seven knots. If the crew got used to sailing a more stable boat, the 60-footers were going to feel squirrely. Best to establish the maximum fright level with the trainers. "You would have to try hard to capsize a conventional Formula 40 in eight to

The boats Stars & Stripes acquired had a mast height of 63′, a beam of 24′, and a sail area of 967 square feet. After Conner got through with them, the numbers read: 83′; 18′6″; 1350 square feet.

Conner dumped one of the 40s in front of the San Diego Yacht Club on May 15, 1988—Opening Day—in just seven knots of breeze. The boss took it in good spirits. A hatch had been left open, causing the "down" hull to sink. It took several boats and twenty people seven hours to right the 40. Up and running again (page opposite). Note the angle of mast rotation.

ten knots of breeze," MacLane says. "The modified boats could flip all too easily. You couldn't go to sleep for a second out there."

Conner's seat-of-the-pants, freewheeling approach to the Formula 40s was instructive to all concerned, himself included. The expendability of the boats allowed for radical experimentation that wouldn't be possible in a more regulated situation. "I learned a lot from what we did with the 40s," Gino Morelli said. "For one thing, with all the extra sail area and reduced beam, the boats went slower upwind."

The Formula 40s provided a good training experience. These turbo-charged terrors tested the cat sailors, and quickly taught the monohull guys respect for the equipment. After sailing the 40s, the bigger boats were faster and more impressive, but tame by comparison.

★

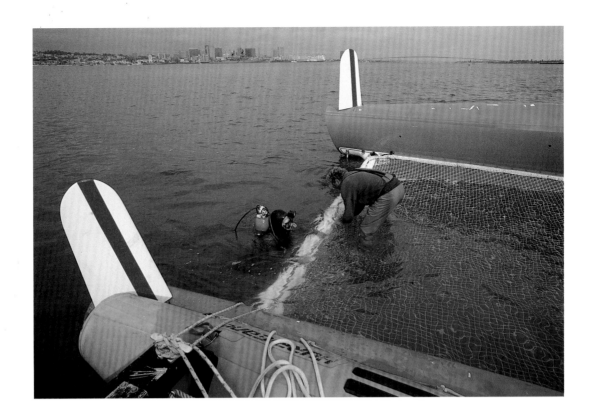

Pierre LeMaout (page opposite) was at the helm one puffy June afternoon when his 40 capsized in the main channel. A guest on board was a split second too slow releasing the gennaker sheet. The rig was cut away, and mast and sails went to the bottom (45 feet down) where diver Mike Schneider (top) retrieved them with air bags. Recovery time for boat and rig: three hours.

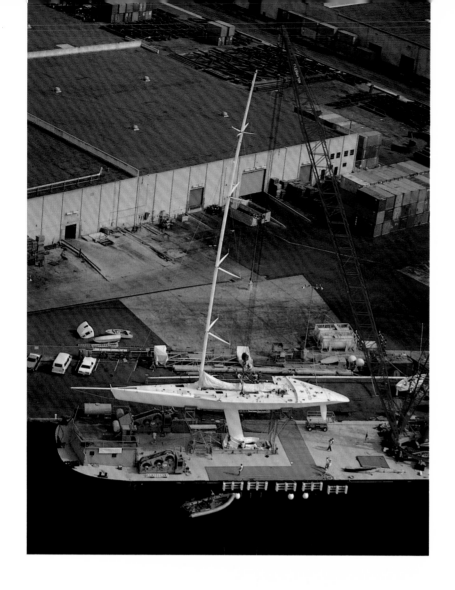

New Zealand arrived in May to begin testing in San Diego. The New Zealand operations base was only a stone's throw south of the Stars & Stripes compound. Conner conceded the crane war to Fay, but nothing else. Page opposite: the big boat sailing against the San Diego waterfront scene became a familiar sight.

SPONSORSHIP
SPONSORSHIP
SPONSORSHIP

Corporate Identity And The Cup

"The Newport Defense in 1983 and the Australian Challenge in 1987—and now San Diego—changed the America's Cup dramatically from a sport that attracted only participants to a popular, broader-based event that attracts sponsors."

William Campbell
Executive V.P. Marketing
Philip Morris USA

America's Cup participation has always required big money. It cost $30,000 to build *America* in 1850, and more cash was required to support her trans-Atlantic passage and the campaign in Great Britain. Those founding, nattily-attired America's Cup backers probably spent the equivalent of $4 million to bring the Auld Mug to the United States.

Cup defenses and challenges have always had backers. Many of the early Cup aspirants—men like T.O.M. Sopwith and Thomas Lipton—funded the campaigns out of pocket, or through personally held companies that enjoyed the resulting publicity and product identity. (Lipton Tea's popularity in America is a case in point.) In the U.S., Harold Vanderbilt and J.P. Morgan paid a lion's share of the cost of defending the Cup.

Later on, small syndicates of wealthy men formed to underwrite and oversee the campaigns. Then in the 1970s, the pinch was felt. Syndicates got larger, and fund raising of a general nature became an important part of participating in the America's Cup.

As the 1980s began, the Cup found itself in a peculiar state. The endless string of U.S. Cup victories had produced ennui even among devotees of the sport. Since 1958 when post-war Cup competition commenced in 12 Meter sloops, the U.S. selection trials consistently produced the best racing. Many of the Cup matches themselves had been downright boring. Interest in the event was flagging, and money for playing the game was tighter than ever. Some wondered if the steady stream of challengers might dry up. Others began to explore new sources of funding without notable success.

Then, in 1983, Australia removed the Cup from its eternal resting place at the New York Yacht Club and whisked it 12,000 miles away. In a stroke, the Cup was elevated to a Holy Grail of sport. Holy Grails require quests, and sponsors love a quest. Five American syndicates were able to find sufficient corporate sponsor-

D.C. Sports marketing specialists Dave McGuigan (left) and John Acton on the way to a call. Uncertainty created by Mercury Bay's sudden, offbeat challenge and the continual litigation that followed made sponsorship difficult to sell.

"We couldn't say
where or when
the event would be."

ship (augmented by private contributions) to send challenging yachts and crews on the very expensive trek to Western Australia. In the end, over 200 international companies used Fremantle and the excitement of America's Cup XXVI as a successful platform for the display of their products and corporate images. ESPN televised much of the live action back to the U.S. The programming was award-winning, the audience ratings beyond ESPN's wildest expectations. America's Cup sponsorship had been born in a big way.

The nature of Michael Fay's 1987 challenge threw sponsorship a curve ball. Both the size of his boat and his method of funding took a page from the past. New Zealand would accept donations of goods and services, but Fay would pay the bills himself. The suddenness of his challenge and the continuing uncertainty it caused clearly illustrated his cavalier view of sponsorship.

"The more things got stirred up with court battles and disagreements, the worse it was for us," John Acton said. Acton and Dave McGuigan, marketing experts from Dennis Conner Sports, went into a sponsorship fire drill the minute Fay's challenge was received. Working alongside Conner, who was making the high-level calls, Acton and McGuigan began frequenting corporate chambers and making presentations. It was a big job. In the past, syndicate frameworks were set up for local efforts. Conner, Acton and McGuigan were on a national canvass.

"We had no video, not even any colorful boards," Acton says. "We would just visit a potential sponsor and talk the story. Then we would have to tell them we couldn't say when the event would be, or whether it would be the best of three or four races, or even where it would be." While the Cup battle raged in and out of court, Fay held tenaciously to a September 19 race date as a bargaining chip. Because of the conflict with the Olympics, that would have been terrible for TV, unattractive for sponsors. "The basic response from sponsors was great," Dave McGuigan says, "but there were no finished deals for a long time. Companies were dragging their feet, and with good reason."

Then Pepsi-Cola joined the campaign in January, 1988, and all the hard work began to pay off. At the end, Stars & Stripes had three major sponsors—Marlboro and Merrill Lynch in addition to Pepsi—who provided a majority of the funds. Louis Vuitton underwrote the Media Center. There were 23 Official Suppliers who provided a combination of cash donations and products; and 38 companies or corporations who donated products to the Stars & Stripes effort.

The most critical aspect of sponsor fulfillment, the display of corporate logos on hulls and sails, was made possible by a relaxation of IYRU Rule #26. When Stars & Stripes rounded the weather mark in race #1 and set a gennaker bearing the Diet Pepsi logo, it was the first time in the 137-year history of the America's Cup that an advertisement had been displayed on any part of a participating vessel. The following day, king size Marlboro and Merrill Lynch logos appeared on the wing sail.

★

Pepsi-Cola executive Michael Lorelli introduces Dennis Conner at the January, 1988, press conference held to announce Pepsi's sponsorship of Stars & Stripes.

"Dennis Conner tracked me down in a Florida hotel in December 1987 and posted me on the court ruling. Within ten minutes we shook hands over the phone.

Defending the Cup, particularly in this ambush attack situation is a very worthwhile American cause. The Pepsi-Cola Company believes in "putting something back." We wanted to help Dennis keep the Cup in America where it belongs. And we knew Dennis would win. He's so committed, driven, dedicated, and resourceful that we knew he would deliver the goods. Dennis Conner and Pepsi are very much alike. We stand for the same things.

We're on the leading edge together: Dennis in the way he approaches race boat technology, and Pepsi in the way we approach marketing. The Cup fits in with our "Big Event Marketing" strategy, like our sponsorship of the Tyson fight.

The American people give Pepsi license to be a little crazy. They expect fun things from us. We take advantage of it. It's OK as long as it's tasteful, like our treatment of the Cup sponsorship. It was consistent with the seriousness of the event, yet fun-loving as Americans have come to know Pepsi."

Michael K. Lorelli
Executive Vice President, Marketing
Pepsi-Cola USA

OFFICIAL SPONSORS

Marlboro
Merrill Lynch & Co., Inc.
Pepsi-Cola U.S.A.

OFFICIAL SUPPLIERS

American Airlines
America's Cup Challenge
ARCO
Atlas Hotels and Travel Services
BASF Structural Materials, Inc.
Eastman Kodak Company
Great American First Savings Bank
Hewlett-Packard
International Marine Industries
Los Angeles Times
Moët-Hennessy
Motorola
Mount Gay Rum
Nautica Apparel
Pizza Hut, Inc.
Rolex Watch U.S.A., Inc.
Science Applications International Corporation
Scott Paper Company
Siemens Information Systems, Inc.
Sperry Top-Sider, Inc.
3M
Toshiba America, Inc., Information Systems Division
Xerox

MEDIA CENTER

Louis Vuitton

We participated in a small way in the Australian Challenge. After that, we got to know Dennis Conner. He's good at public relations. You have to appreciate how he brought this sport to the public. Those of us who know Dennis, his personal story, understand how he can translate the sport of the rich into a sport that many people can identify with. People in the street now talk about grinders and tailers the way they talk about running backs and tight ends.

It's unfortunate that this defense was tied up with businessmen's wrangles. But as I sense people's enthusiasm for this event, it gives me great hope that the Cup will continue to broaden its appeal.

I hope the United States can stage a defense that will capture people's imaginations like in Australia. There is a wonderful carnival atmosphere that can be created around the Cup that is more in line with what traditionally appeals to sponsors.

William Campbell
Executive V.P. Marketing
Philip Morris USA

Philip Morris executive William Campbell.

Conner is flanked by Merrill Lynch executives Daniel Tully (left), and William Schreyer.

We at Merrill Lynch are proud to continue our sponsorship of Stars & Stripes and of our long-standing association with the America's Cup. Our firm's sponsorship of the world's premier yachting event is in keeping with a tradition of support for sporting, cultural and civic programs in the U.S. and around the world.

In 1983, Merrill Lynch was sole financial services sponsor of the America's Cup races in Newport, R.I. Four years later we helped Dennis Conner and his crew recapture the Cup in Fremantle, Western Australia. Now Stars & Stripes has met the challenge from New Zealand, again demonstrating the best of American ingenuity, technological expertise, and sailing prowess.

We like to think we share Dennis Conner's philosophy: that with vision, preparation, and courage, you can be the best at what you do. We admire those who look beyond the everyday and the ordinary to achieve greatness.

Once again we salute Dennis Conner, the crew, and the entire Stars & Stripes team. We're proud of their determined and successful efforts to keep the Cup in America.

William A. Schreyer
Chairman and
Chief Executive Officer

Daniel P. Tully
President and
Chief Operating Officer

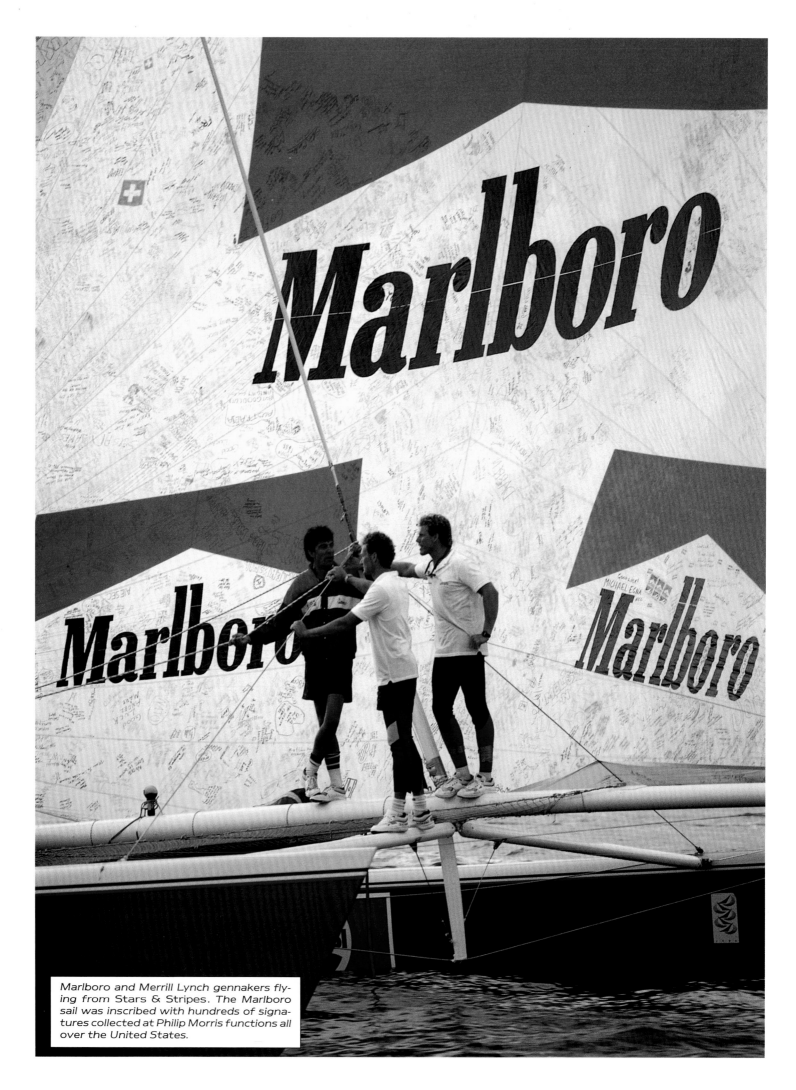

Marlboro and Merrill Lynch gennakers flying from Stars & Stripes. The Marlboro sail was inscribed with hundreds of signatures collected at Philip Morris functions all over the United States.

WINGS

Wingmaster Dana Timmer banks his airplane over the Mojave.

Stand a winglet on end, mount it vertically on a wing tip (below), and it provides cleaner airflow, a more efficient flight for the Long-eze airplane that pilot and sailor Dana Timmer built. Stand a large wing on end, mount it on a multihull, and it becomes a sail. Vertical or horizontal, a wing's job is the same: to provide lift. On a sailboat, the force generated by any sail combines with the force generated by hulls, daggerboards, and rudders to drive the boat forward.

Wing sails have been powering boats with increasing success since the early 1970s when it was discovered that light, easily-driven multihulls were compatible with the great potential of these "hard" wing sails. The faster a boat moves, the more efficient the wing becomes and the more power it produces. A wing sail performs quietly, without the luffing of sail cloth, and without the heavy tackle that's required to tension the leech of a soft sail. The leech of a wing sail stands on its own.

Heavier displacement monohulls have hull speed limitations that preclude a wing sail's great potential. Con-

In the spirit. Sign hung in the shop at SCI indicates that the desert-bound airplane builders have turned into enthusiastic sailmakers.

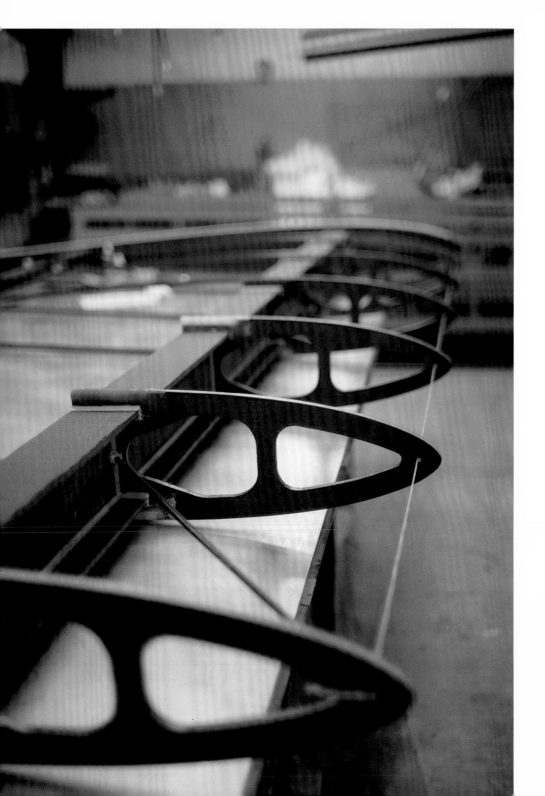

ventional (soft) sails effectively fill the monohull's needs, although wing sails could possibly be developed for ultra-light monohulls of the future.

Until 1988, the largest wing sail designed and built was for a 25-foot, C-Class catamaran. It had an area of 300 square feet, and was 37.5 feet tall. The serious consideration of a catamaran by the Stars & Stripes design team was accompanied by an influx of multihull experts with wings on their minds. "Wing nuts." Faced with the notion of a 60-foot catamaran, they envisioned a wing of staggering proportions. They began with the C-Class wing, a known quantity, expanding and modifying with new shapes and concepts until they had drawn a wing 89 feet tall with a sail area of 1320 square feet. It was 2.25 times the size of its C-Class relative.

Who would build such a wing? Scaled Composites, Inc., the company that built *Voyager* (the plane that circled the globe non-stop), stepped forward to do the job. SCI was founded by airplane wizard Burt Rutan, its president. Stars & Stripes' own wing nuts moved to the desert to help on the job.

It was built in only 12 weeks and it was a spectacular wing, breath-taking to all who gazed upon it. Constructed of a carbon fiber laminate over honeycomb,

Two workers at SCI transfer an airfoil pattern to a block of foam in the process of making a mold. Carbon fiber frames fabricated for the sail's third element (below and left opposite) await the next step in the building process. At right, below, are sections of the second element.

A Giant Among Wing Sails

the wing weighed only 1400 pounds—400 pounds less than the soft rig—and it worked perfectly. Rigged on the boat, the wing cut a strange, compelling figure sailing on the Harbor. But after a month of trials, the sailors decided that it wasn't big enough. More power was needed. Back to the futuristic drawing board (the Computer Assisted Design System), and back to Scaled Composites went the wing nuts, with plans for a new wing sail that would dwarf even the 100-foot mast on the soft rig cat.

Only eight weeks later (!), with 25 people working 65 hours a week, a new and bigger wing was ready. It was a true giant among wing sails, perhaps the biggest that will be built for many years to come. It has a sail area of 1860 square feet, it is 107 feet tall, and it weighs 2000 pounds. The new wing sail also worked perfectly, and proved virtually trouble-free.

"It was an engineering textbook exercise," Dave Hubbard says with some pride. "Design, engineering, and construction consumed 99% of the total time spent. Maintenance, alteration, and repair took only 1%. The crew never lost a day of sailing because of the wing."

A worker sands element #1, the wing sail's "mast." Below, the 107-foot wing sail mast is laid out on the shop floor at SCI amid the plant's more usual occupants.

Builders' signatures near the top of the first wing sail. A final, 15-foot section designed to break away in a capsize was attached to this plate. The sail could theoretically be "reefed" by removing this top section prior to launching. Several watertight compartments were incorporated into both wing sails to provide buoyancy if needed.

Finishing one of the two "shark fin" winglets that would be set atop the larger wing sail. The winglets were designed to reduce turbulence at the top of the sail. Below, finished sections of element #2 await assembly. Their function was to regulate the size of the slot between element #1 (the mast), and element #2 (the trailing edge flaps).

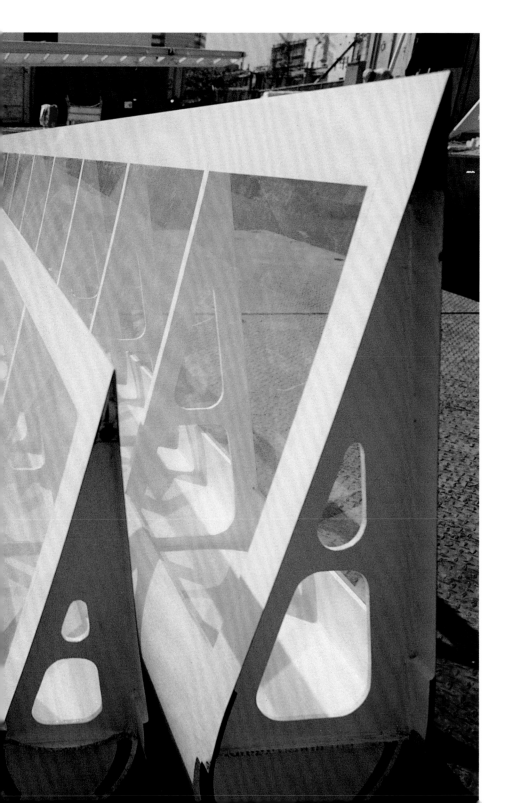

The wing in place (opposite page), showing control arms and wires that adjusted the position of element #3 (far left). At right, putting the finishing touches on the heat-shrink plastic covering of element #1, which is lying horizontal with the leading edge down. The clear windows were light weight, and made for easy visual inspection of control wires. Below, the wing horizontal with the trailing edge (leech) nearest the camera. The foot of the sail is to the left.

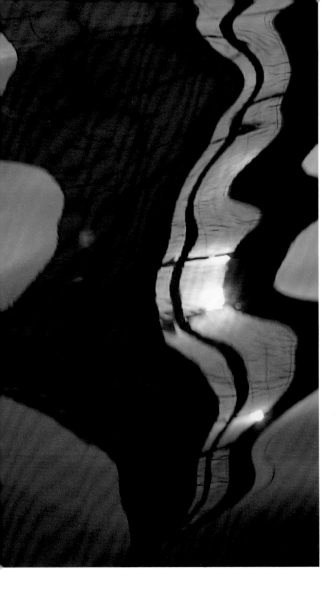

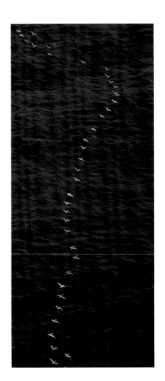

The launching of US-1 (page opposite). Below, Dana Timmer crosses wings with the cat off Point Loma.

US-1

SAILING

Taming Two Bad Cats

With the hulls still wrapped for shipping, the cat is raised upright after being tilted to receive element #1 of the wing sail. Below, front view of a hull's knife-edged stem.

The two 60-foot catamarans arrived from the builder, R.D. Boat Works, on May 19. The boats were in pieces, of course, and unpainted. The wing arrived from Scaled Composites a few days later. That too had to be assembled and rigged with control wires and scores of tiny strain gauges that required thousands of feet of wire. The mast for the soft sail arrived as well, all 100-feet of it. Erecting that was standard procedure, but the wing needed special handling. A custom hydraulic tilt bed was fabricated to be the winged cat's cradle.

The "flipmobile" tilted the boat 90 degrees, allowing the wing to be stored horizontal behind the windbreak of containers three levels high. The flipmobile was also used to rig the wing. The wing was first laid out horizontal at the proper height. The cat was tilted 90 degrees to receive it, then tilted upright, the wing having been secured in place on its titanium mast step with shrouds and stays. The tilt system worked flawlessly, but it never failed to frighten those who were watching the operation for the first time. ☆

Sidewalk superintendents watch the cat being tilted. From left, Dennis Conner, Peter Isler, Chris Bedford, naval architect Karl Kirkman, Rich McCurdy, and Rowena Carlson. Page opposite: Conner takes a close look at his new catamaran.

A clutch of San Diego Yacht Club commodores and their wives examines the wing sail of their Cup defender. From left, Mrs. Douglas Alford, Commodore Fred Frye, Commodore Alford, Mrs. Ben McKesson, and Commodore McKesson. Page opposite: a fish-eye view of the wing sail catamaran, with the wing's co-designer Dave Hubbard stretched upon the trampoline netting under the wing's trimming mechanism.

Conner speaks during the commissioning of Stars & Stripes 88 at the San Diego Yacht Club on June 5th. Applauding are (from left) Mrs. Douglas Alford, Commodore Alford, Malin and Roberta Burnham.

US-1
Designer: Sail America Design Team

l.o.a.	60 ft.
l.w.l.	55 ft.
beam	30 ft.
w.l. beam	29.2 ft.
displacement	6,500 lbs.
mast height	104 ft.
sail area	1,900 sq. ft.

On a gorgeous San Diego 4th of June, 1988, 30,000 people turned out at B Street Pier (above) to witness the christening of *Stars & Stripes*, the catamaran. The soft rig boat stood in for both cats, since it is impossible to secure a wing sail boat to a dock without it wanting to fly. ESPN's Jim Kelly was master of ceremonies for a distinguished delegation that included California Governor George Deukmejian and his wife. Two F-14 fighters made a sensational low pass over the gathering as Mrs. Deukmejian and Mrs. Douglas Alford simultaneously whacked special break-away bottles of champagne over both delicate bows. Thousands of balloons were released, the band played, and on the water, the wing cat thrilled the crowd with a surprise sail-by. Watching it

pass in the congested waters off the B Street Pier, with one hull flying high, John Marshall was heard to mutter, "Take it easy with that thing."

The next day there was a well-attended private commissioning ceremony at the San Diego Yacht Club. Some of the Club's America's Cup history was on display in the form of three boats docked in front of the clubhouse (below): *Liberty* (left), the formerly red boat in which Dennis Conner lost to the Australians in 1983; *Stars & Stripes 87* (right), the boat in which Conner won the Cup back in 1987; and *Stars & Stripes 88*, the catamaran defender, at center stage.

"Fay has a formidable boat," Conner told the audience. "We don't take this challenge lightly. Ours will be a 100% effort." ☆

An on-board view of the wing (page opposite), a dramatic and new look in mainsails. Above, the conventional soft rig boat leaps off a Pacific roller. For their light weight and spidery appearance, the catamarans were deceptively tough.

Going to weather at 14 knots or so in a breeze, flying spray stung faces and hands. The speed of the boats was breathtaking. The ride was thrilling, rough, and very wet.

Gino Morelli hanks on the jib.

Taking a break: John Wake, Bill Trenkle, John Barnitt, Rambo, and Cam Lewis (back to camera), share a joke, while Gino Morelli reclines on a bow strut.

Conner steers the soft rig during trials held in August to select the fastest cat. As in the past, Conner often steered the slower boat by choice for the challenge it offered.

The winged cat displays a slim profile.

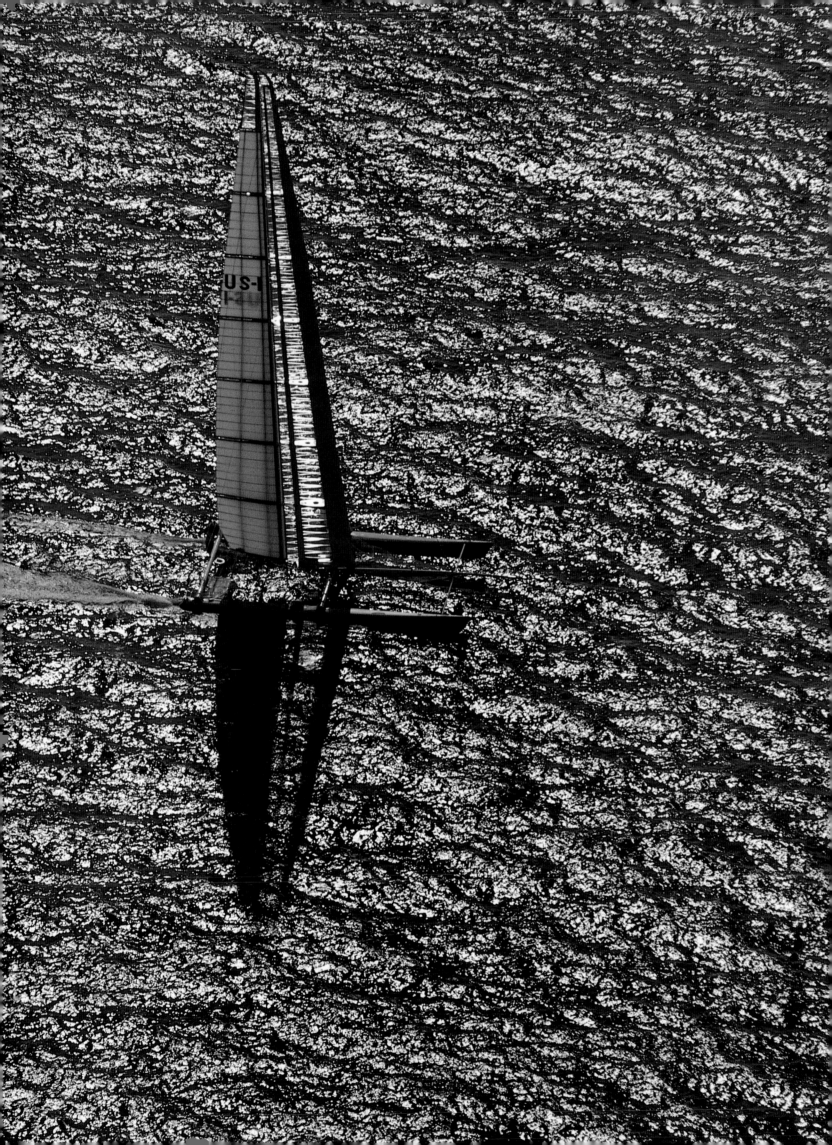

The wing cat (page opposite) sails a sea of
pounded silver. Above, the soft rig under full sail.
Following page, Stars & Stripes flies a hull as she
sails past the carrier USS Enterprise, which visited
San Diego on a liberty call in July, 1988.

SAILING

The

Big

Boat

The view from the mast tip of New Zealand (KZ-1), as a passing power boat turns for a closer look at the giant sloop. Page opposite, The Big Boat on a tear, with the foredeck crew getting ready for a sail change.

Flying one of her giant gennakers, New Zealand makes knots off the wind. Bowsprit problems (below) plagued New Zealand all summer. Here the crew sorts out the tangle of wires controlling the articulating bowsprit, which was eventually scrapped for a fixed one.

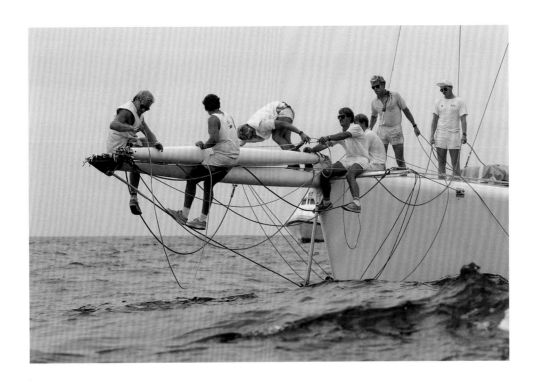

In light air, most of New Zealand's crew of 35 would sit on the leeward wing.

Eight of The Big Boat's crew was always below deck, lined up on cross-connected coffee grinders used for hauling up sails and trimming the big gennakers.

View from the lee quarter showing the twin wheels
and the immense span of the 26 foot-wide deck.
Note the instrument readouts aft of the mast, and
the length of the traveler track.

SAILING

High Tech

Meteorologist Chris Bedford, veteran of the 1987 campaign, found the Pacific much friendlier than the Indian Ocean. But he still started work at 5AM. Why? "I could miss something."

Stars & Stripes' scientific team on location. From left, Clay Oliver, Jay Rossen, Dick McCurdy, and Rowena Carison (seated).

Dick McCurdy, of Ockam Instruments, designed and wrote the programs. Jay Rossen built and maintained the systems, and Rowena Carlson managed the four powerful computers that processed all weather data and boat telemetry (wind speed, boat speed, wind direction, VMG, etc.). One computer could be detached and taken to Point Loma in a van to collect data while the boats were sailing. At day's end it would be returned to the compound and "dump" its data into the main system. In Fremantle, that data transfer took 90 minutes. In 1988, it took just 25 seconds.

Permissions for land use and access to frequencies—including one from AMTRAK—filled a large notebook. The wide open cats were rough on sensitive instruments, but in the end the systems worked, McCurdy was pleased. "We might never have a chance like this again," he said. "The potential of these boats is incredible. We've come a long way in learning why they work."

Dick McCurdy displays his smallest computer.

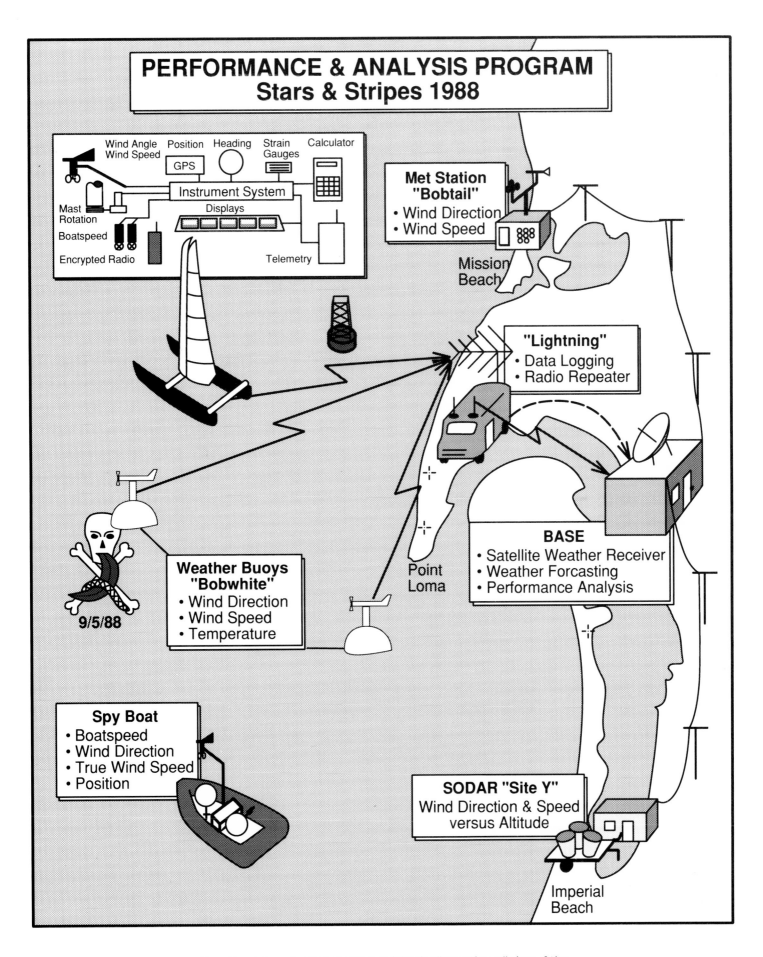

PERFORMANCE & ANALYSIS PROGRAM
Stars & Stripes 1988

Wind Angle / Wind Speed · Position · Heading · Strain Gauges · Calculator

GPS

Instrument System

Mast Rotation

Displays

Boatspeed

Encrypted Radio

Telemetry

Met Station "Bobtail"
• Wind Direction
• Wind Speed

Mission Beach

"Lightning"
• Data Logging
• Radio Repeater

Weather Buoys "Bobwhite"
• Wind Direction
• Wind Speed
• Temperature

9/5/88

Point Loma

BASE
• Satellite Weather Receiver
• Weather Forcasting
• Performance Analysis

Spy Boat
• Boatspeed
• Wind Direction
• True Wind Speed
• Position

SODAR "Site Y"
Wind Direction & Speed versus Altitude

Imperial Beach

How the data collection worked. "Lightning" was the call sign of the computer van that parked daily at Point Loma. Data came in from the catamarans and two weather buoys, one of which disappeared on 9/5/88, at 3:30 AM. The van was also linked to the compound base, which was wired to two shore-based meteorological stations. Chart courtesy of Dick McCurdy.

JUDGEMENT

More Postponement Than Decision

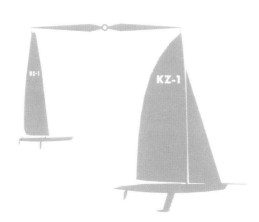

Justice Carmen Beauchamp Ciparick presides.

"The Time Has Come For The Sailors To Participate..."

When Design Team Director John Marshall announced on January 22, 1988, that two catamarans would be built for the defense of America's Cup XXVII, a controversy started that had not been concluded by the time this book went to press in October, 1988. *Stars & Stripes* won the America's Cup on the water. But because of pending legal action, the Cup itself was not awarded.

"At first Fay thought we wouldn't be able to raise the money to defend," Marshall said. "We had very little time, no community support—he thought he had us on the mat. Then by spring, Pepsi, Marlboro, and Merrill Lynch had become Official Sponsors, and we had boats and a wing sail under construction. We were sailing daily in the Formula 40s. Fay's boat was sailing too, and he began to see his own problems: a 40-man crew, no trial horse, a keel without enough lateral resistance, and

Sail America partisans pose on the steps of The New York Supreme Court. From left, Tom Ehman, Mark Smith, Ken Poovey, Doug Alford, and John Marshall.

he figured the best way out might be a lawsuit."

In a brief filed in May, 1988, with the Supreme Court of the State of New York, the challenger (Mercury Bay Boating Club) contended that San Diego would be in contempt if S.D.Y.C. arrived at the starting line to defend the America's Cup in a multihull vessel or other boat not "like and similar" to the challenging yacht, *New Zealand.* ("Like and similar" is a phrase Michael Fay used repeatedly from the time he first took issue with the multihull. He gave the impression he was quoting from some official document related to the Deed of Gift. Such was not the case. "The first time I saw that phrase was in a press release issued by Fay in December," says Sail America's attorney Mark Smith, of Latham & Watkins. "There is no question that the Mercury Bay side coined it.")

Eight weeks passed before Justice Carmen Beauchamp Ciparick announced her decision, which was more a postponement than a ruling on the matter.

"To determine the boat issue at

this time would be to render a largely meaningless advisory opinion," Ciparick wrote, one that " ... would countenance continued bickering, and encourage further litigation which would inevitably delay commencement of the races. ... This court cannot be used by the parties to obtain preliminary rulings on issues of naval architecture. ... Nothing in this decision should be interpreted as indicating that multihulled boats are either permitted or barred under the America's Cup deed of gift. ... The vision that Schuyler and the other donors sought to perpetuate over the years was that of an international race on a grand scale between boats on the seas and not a landbound battle among clever lawyers in the courthouse."

In conclusion, Ciparick wrote: "The time has come for the sailors to be permitted to participate in the America's Cup. The parties are directed to proceed with the races and to reserve their protests, if any, until after completion of the America's Cup races." The cloud of uncertainty remained, but at least the

John Cox Stephens

not only knew

about multihulls,

he owned one.

races could proceed.

For San Diego Yacht Club, Sail America, and Stars & Stripes—proponents of the multihull—Ciparick's decree to go race was something of a victory, and it was hard won. Forseeing Fay's objection, San Diego began substantiating its right to defend in a multihull way back in December, 1987. At that time two groups began gathering information that would support both historical and legal precedent for a multihull.

Ed du Moulin, manager of several defense syndicates since the 1970s, and a long-time Conner supporter, and Harman Hawkins, attorney for the New York Yacht Club over the years, began preparing a "white paper" on the legal aspects of a multihull Cup defender.

Meanwhile, Marshall assembled a team to research the papers of Cup founder George Schuyler, and prepare a brief history of multihulls. Led by Marshall and Belgian-born America's Cup historian Daniel Charles, the group included former *New York Times* yachting writer Joanne Fishman, who had been Conner's press agent in 1983; and *Freedom* and *Liberty* navigator Halsey Herreshoff, yacht designer and curator of the Herreshoff museum in Bristol, R.I.

"We learned a lot of interesting things," John Marshall says. "*America*'s challenge, how she took American naval technology to the trade exposition in England, was uncovered in a major way. Her design was totally different, a threat to the British."

When it came to multihulls, there were several surprises. John Cox Stephens, a founder of the New York Yacht Club and one of *America*'s backers, commissioned seven boats in his lifetime. Each was considered radical, having been conceived upon an innovative principle of naval architecture. One of Stephens' boats, *Maria*, the largest sloop of her day (116 feet), had movable ballast. Another (1820) was a catamaran called *Double Trouble*. "Here was the man behind the founding spirit of the Cup fascinated by design innovation," Marshall says. "He not only knew about multihulls, he owned one."

The research was exhaustive. It dug into the futuristic multihull designs of Nathanial Herreshoff drawn in the late 1800s—light boats with articulating hulls—and documented early monohull-multihull disputes. One involved a catamaran named *Nereid* (1877) that the New York Yacht Club tried to exclude from racing. The owner reminded the members of the club's purpose as cited in the charter: " ... encouraging yacht building and naval architecture and the cultivation of naval science." The Commodore called *Nereid* "an abomination," but the boat was awarded a certificate and admitted to the fleet. (It was a slow boat that consistently finished poorly.) "We found a model of *Neried* on the wall at the New York Yacht Club," Marshall says. "So Schuyler had to know about that boat and the argument that surrounded it. If he wanted to legislate against catamarans in the Deed, he would have done so."

"The Deed presents a comprehensible set of rules," Marshall says. "It promotes open design. The winner simply finds the fastest boat of a given length. There were no one-designs in those days. Multihulls won, and so did monohulls."

Sail America wasn't the only one doing homework and making a case about the decision to pit a multihull defender against a monohull. The controversy spread throughout the sport. Most of the world's sailing magazines published opinions on the subject, and there wasn't a yacht club bar where the issue wasn't discussed. The Deed of Gift was suddenly on everyone's reading list. Amid all the debate, there was probably only one consensus: the multihull might be legal, but racing it against a monohull would make for an unusual contest.

By the time Mercury Bay Boating Club filed a motion on May 4, 1988, asking the New York Supreme Court to find the San Diego Yacht Club in contempt for its multihull defender, Sail America's research was completed and on the back burner. With only two weeks to file a brief in response, John Marshall dropped his other duties and went into daily sessions with attorneys Ken Poovey and Mark Smith from the San Diego office of Latham & Watkins. Joining them was Sandy Benson, Poovey's assistant.

"There was barely time to read the Mercury Bay material," Mark Smith says. "Including affidavits and exhibits, it was 6 inches thick and over 1000 pages." The material arrived when Smith was hospitalized, recuperating from surgery.

Attorneys Mark Smith (left) and Ken Poovey flank Poovey's assistant Sandy Benson. Benson cradles Sail America's paperwork, while Smith and Poovey heft some of Mercury Bay's submissions which numbered well over 1000 pages.

New Zealand's attorney didn't know the difference between a keel and a centerboard.

"I read it through a Demerol haze, which made it more intelligible," Smith says.

In a week's time a draft of the Sail America brief had been written in San Diego. On May 13th, the four flew to New York to begin another frenzied week of work that would leave little time for sleep. On the 14th, they arranged to argue their case before a moot court of three former judges who had been hired for the purpose. Having a mock hearing was a creative notion, one Marshall says turned out to be very productive.

For the next five days, Benson, Marshall, Poovey and Smith were closeted in Latham & Watkins' New York office writing a final draft of the brief. They also worked on the telephone to reach a variety of far-flung experts, two of whom had given affidavits to New Zealand that discredited the multihull. The object was to cross-examine these experts, present them with the San Diego arguments, and convince them to write additional statements more favorable to the multi-hull concept. In this effort John Marshall says they had considerable success.

The hearing before Justice Ciparick was on May 25. New Zealand, as plaintiff, was first to argue. "New Zealand's brief was weak in substance," Marshall says, "and their attorney proved several times he didn't know the difference between a keel and a centerboard. But they came on strong with moral argument."

Next was Royal Burnham Yacht Club from Great Britain, which was seeking to intervene (with status from an earlier petition filed before the Court), to enforce a challenger elimination series. Royal Burnham's contender, a foil-assisted creation named *Blue Arrow*, had been built on the assumption it would be allowed to race.

"Having Royal Burnham appear next was a great plus for us," Marshall says. "The Royal Burnham attorney is a great speaker. He told the court that New Zealand had essentially been lying when they said they would welcome other competition. He said New Zealand's 'yes' had quickly turned into a 'maybe,' and finally a 'no' when it was clear that Royal Burnham's yacht wasn't equal to or slower than New Zealand's challenger. So the British effectively undercut New Zealand's moral position."

It was two months later to the day when Justice Ciparick issued her "go race" decree.

When the racing was over, there was speculation that Michael Fay might simply accept the loss and regroup for the next challenge. Fay had been adamant in interviews just prior to and following race #1 that he would be returning to court after the event. Was he just playing out his litigious scenario? Not at all. On September 13, as Fay made arrangements for his big boat to tour several east coast U.S. cities in conjunction with the grand opening of a Fay/Richwhite office in Manhattan, Mercury Bay attorney George Tompkins wrote Justice Ciparick requesting a conference.

"There was no motion, no petition, no brief filed," Mark Smith said, "which meant nothing relating to the Cup remained on the court's docket. The old case was finished, given that the time for appeal had run out." But the conference was granted for Wednesday, October 12, at 2:30 P.M. in Ciparick's chambers. Invited were San Diego Yacht Club, the New York Attorney General, and representatives of New York and Royal Perth Yacht Clubs. As Smith said, it was curious.

For those in doubt at the time about Mercury Bay's intentions, a flat assessment came from an insider, one of Fay's lieutenants from the New Zealand compound. When asked about what new legal action might be taken, the lieutenant shrugged and said that Michael Fay's America's Cup had begun right after the last race concluded.

Michael Fay, the first man in America's Cup history to take a challenge to court, photographed on the steps of The New York Supreme Court.

A Boat Race At Last

Justice Ciparick's decision on July 25 put the sailors back in America's Cup XXVII. Never mind that the designers and attorneys had stolen the scene, or that a rout was in the offing. At last there would be a boat race. A best two-of-three-race series would begin at noon, Pacific Daylight Time, on Wednesday, September 7, 1988.

For the eight weeks prior to Ciparick's decision, the two camps had been going doggedly through the motions of getting ready—sail testing, repairing gear, making modifications, sanding and painting and grinding—when the nagging question in their minds was this: "Ready for what?" All through the winter, spring, and into the summer months of 1988, millions of dollars and untold man hours had been spent by both sides for an America's Cup race that might become a fantasy. On many a day weariness born of uncertainty was the biggest obstacle for both crews.

Now, finally, the race was on. Two of the more incredible racing machines of their kind ever designed and built would be on display before the world. For both teams the challenge was to perform with flawless seamanship and plenty of finesse—to make the best possible showing. ☆

Skipper Conner aboard Stars & Stripes listens as tactician Tom Whidden makes a point.

New Zealand skipper David Barnes is flanked by teammates. At left, the crew of the big boat always exercised prior to sailing. Below, Conner announces his team at the Louis Vuitton Media Center. From left: Tom Whidden; Peter Isler; Carl Buchan; Cam Lewis; Bill Trenkle; Duncan MacLane; John Barnitt; John Wake; John Grant; Randy Smyth; Skip Banks.

New Zealander Chris Dickson steering the winged cat at Conner's invitation. Dickson skippered Kiwi Magic in the 1987 Louis Vuitton Challenge Trials in Australia.

John Marshall shows how he really feels about the new, improved, extra-large wing sail.

Conner with Jack Sutphen in a light moment at the compound. Sutphen moved to San Diego from the East Coast eight years ago to work with Conner's racing programs.

126

New York Yacht Club Commodore Frank Snyder, Sail America Trustee Bill Packer, and Conner confer beneath the wing sail cat resting on the flipmobile.

International Judges Cy Gillette (left) and Mort Bloom flank Ed du Moulin.

As the Stars & Stripes campaign peaked for the upcoming match, activity at the compound accelerated. There were many new but familiar faces in evidence. New York Yacht Club Commodore Frank Snyder arrived in San Diego to confer about the Cup's future and stopped by the compound to have a look at the catamarans. Veteran Conner campaigner Ed du Moulin arrived from New York to pitch in and pick up loose ends. Former ocean racer and IYRU Judge Cy Gillette flew in from Hawaii to assist with preparation in case of a protest. And Mort Bloom, another IYRU Judge, came down from Marina Del Ray to be Stars & Stripes' representative on the race committee boat. Spit and polish was liberally applied around the compound, and security was tightened a notch. Meanwhile, Conner was continuing to take dignitaries and friends sailing on the catamaran a week before the Cup. The mood was generally light and confident as race day approached.

Conner with Malin Burnham. The two have been partners in the America's Cup game since 1980.

"Live, From San Diego..."

Once again the media arrived en masse to cover America's Cup XXVII. Tom Mitchell, Sail America's Vice President for Communications, reported that 850 media credentials were issued to correspondents from all over the world. Live radio and TV rights were purchased by ESPN, but that didn't stop Detroit's WWJ radio from broadcasting dozens of live interviews from a transmitter atop the Marriott Hotel.

ESPN television, The Total Sports Network, jumped into America's Cup coverage in 1987 in a big way. It paid off. Millions of Americans stayed up half the night watching the event. In 1988, ESPN was back, and with the popular on-camera team of anchor Jim Kelly and color man Gary Jobson. They had excellent help from former *USA* skipper Tom Blackaller, and ace San Diego sportscaster Phil Stone.

Like everyone connected with America's Cup XXVII, ESPN had to shuffle scheduling until the 11th hour. But their commitment to the Cup was made long before that. In June, 1988, they began airing a series of six one-hour historical shows as part of their "Road to the America's Cup" theme. And as early as March, ESPN's technical staff began casing San Diego for what would be one of the most complex television hook-ups ever attempted by a single network.

In addition to their award-winning programming, ESPN had been justifiably proud of their technical accomplishment out of Western Australia. But the problems presented by the San Diego coverage would make 1987 seem simple. Filing for available microwave access with the FCC accounted for paperwork an inch thick. As ESPN's technical supervisor Douglas Dodson said, "We're exploring new applications for broadcast technology."

Distance was the major difference. The Fremantle Cup races were sailed on a closed course 3.25 miles in diameter. In San Diego, with the teams unable to agree on a course, the Deed of Gift suggestions were used. Race #1 would be 20 miles to windward and return. Race #2 would be around an equilateral, 13-mile triangle. Simple line of sight telemetry would not be sufficient to send a television signal that far, especially over water, which creates signal-reflection problems.

ESPN solved the problem by using helicopters hovering above cameramen in chase boats to transmit the signal back to receivers atop the Marriott Hotel. By maintaining the proper altitude, the choppers used the high bluff of Point Loma to block ghost signals that were bouncing off the ocean. A camera blimp was on station as well.

Nineteen cameras were set up to cover the event, seven of which were aboard the two race boats. Two of these technological marvels were no bigger than lipsticks. The other five were inside waterproof housings the size of a softball, complete with 180- to 360-degree panning capability, and an assortment of lenses. Not only were the cameras in a hostile environment—especially on the wide-open, spray-pelted catamaran—but everything was remote controlled, and that presented another enormous hurdle. As communications central for the U.S. Navy's Pacific Fleet, San Diego may origi-

nate more radio transmissions than any place on earth. Finding an open frequency is a guessing game, one that Navy security is understandably reluctant to facilitate.

In order to broadcast a picture back to the announce boat 25 miles offshore, so Kelly and Jobson could see what they were talking about, ESPN obtained part-time use of a little-used commercial frequency. From 7PM to 3AM the channel was used for adult programming. Race #1 got off the air with time to spare, but during the post-race tow in, those boats which had been tuned to race coverage were treated to spicier stuff.

Five minutes to air time (11:25 PDT) on September 7, the video signal from the announce boat camera was lost. Kelly and Jobson, ready with the show's opening, were blacked out. From his post in the production truck at the Marriott, live show producer Jed Drake quickly talked through the opening on-camera segment with Phil Stone and Tom Blackaller, who were stationed at a "host set" in Embarcadero Park. Moments later it was "Live, from San Diego...", and America's Cup XXVII was on the air. It was television team work at its best.

Kelly handled the opening voice-over by watching the announce boat monitor, then threw to Phil Stone who caught the ball on-camera and ran smoothly with it, passing to Blackaller along the way. Eighteen minutes later the announce boat video was reconnected. At the 10-minute gun (11:50 AM), Kelly and Jobson were into their pre-race play by play as if nothing had happened.

ESPN's coverage of Race #1 was plagued by a few technical problems. And for some reason, the audio signal from the announce boat effectively disrupted the programming of Radio Tijuana.

By Race #2 on Friday, September 9, almost everything was up and running. The quality of the coverage pleased Jed Drake. "It proved that 1987 wasn't a fluke," he said. "We didn't have enough time to get ready, but we said we could do it and we did." ☆

San Diego cameraman Bob Sloan was a workhorse shooting ESPN Cup features.

Conner at the helm with Tom Whidden, Cam Lewis, and Carl Buchan at work in Race #1. The white, gold-banded globe on the cross beam (foreground) is a remote controlled television camera.

Louis Vuitton turned San Diego's condemned former police station into a media center so handsome the city considered saving it. The facilities included 150 desks, 250 telephone lines, 20 television monitors, a staff of 13, and 33 volunteers.

ESPN's Jim Kelly and Gary Jobson on the announce boat. After an initial blackout, their live coverage sparkled throughout the long afternoon.

Race #1

Race #1. As predicted, Conner stayed away from *New Zealand* at the start. No need courting trouble when you have a faster boat. *New Zealand* was slightly ahead and to leeward at the gun, a good position in 12 Meters but of no value in this contest. The breeze was under 6 knots, the optimum condition for *New Zealand*'s tall rig and huge sails. But the cat quickly showed she could handle it as well. *New Zealand* immediately started a tacking duel, to no avail. After a dozen tacks, *Stars & Stripes* was clearly gaining. The cat tacked as fast, and sailed as high as the big monohull, with a significant speed advantage even in the light air. Once in the lead, Conner had the luxury of being able to stay in phase with the wind shifts, thereby gaining even more on the big boat. With the race only 20 minutes old, barring breakdowns the outcome was evident. Conner sailed his boat conservatively, and still led at the mark by 9:04. His winning margin was 18:15.

☆

The photos on this page were taken aboard Stars & Stripes by crewman Cam Lewis. Prior to the start of Race #1, the cat tracks the big boat. John Wake sits on the bow sprit (left), while Bill Trenkle tends the jib (right), and Tom Whidden (foreground) peers to leeward.

Whidden takes a bearing as Stars & Stripes splits tacks with New Zealand early in Race #1. Point Loma, San Diego's famous headland, is just visible in the background. Even with his speed advantage, Conner stayed close to his opponent in the light conditions. Page opposite: side by side after the start.

Boats of the privileged spectator fleet follow in New Zealand's wake as the big boat chases the catamaran early in Race #1. Stars & Stripes is in mid-tack as Conner applies a loose cover.

Taken forty-five minutes into Race #1, this photograph tells all. Stars & Stripes is directly to weather of New Zealand, sailing on the same or slightly better heading. The privileged fleet is at left. In the distance, the rest of the spectator fleet is barely visible against Point Loma.

Nineteen miles south of Point Loma, almost to the weather mark in Race #1, sailors' luck surfaced in the form of hundreds of dolphins, which toyed with the cat for several minutes. Stars & Stripes was no challenge for these speedy denizens.

The gun flashes as Stars & Stripes crosses the finish line to win Race #1. When the crew raised the Diet Pepsi gennaker as the cat rounded the weather mark, it was the first time in history a sail had carried an advertisement during an America's Cup race.

Race #2

Standing in the bow pulpit of Betsy, Lucy Jewett bids the crew of Stars & Stripes farewell as they depart for Race #2.

Members of New Zealand's cockpit crew can only watch from the rail as Stars & Stripes widens her lead in Race #2.

Race #2 was a triangle of 13-mile legs. Again the wind was under six knots. David Barnes lost the start to Conner by 29 seconds. But then the Kiwis had their best moment. Barnes faked a tack. Conner bought it, and his boat nearly stopped. When Conner tacked back and came after *New Zealand*, Barnes luffed *Stars & Stripes* head to wind, and Conner tacked away. It was a good show by the Kiwis. They effectively slowed the catamaran for 15 minutes of the race. But on the next crossing, *Stars & Stripes* went ahead for the duration. Conner stayed close to *New Zealand*, covering tack for tack in the spotty wind.

Just before 1 PM, the breeze shifted to the right and freshened to 15 knots, with seas building to three feet. With more than enough wind for his big wing sail, Conner dropped his jib for the remainder of the race. *Stars & Stripes* led at the first mark by 10:00; at the second mark by 11:56; and at the finish by 21:10.

A foredeck hand tacks the gennaker to the bowsprit as New Zealand approaches the windward mark in Race #2. It was a great day for sailing. The sun was bright, the air was clear, and the water was legendary Pacific blue. The strong breeze put a bone in the teeth of both boats.

The crew of Stars & Stripes exults as the gun signals the finish of Race #2, the final race of America's Cup XXVII. Below, Conner, Whidden, and Randy Smyth look pleased as they sail home trailed by chase boats and the spectator fleet, which are straining to keep pace with the cat.

The celebration begins. After crossing the line, Conner picked up the remaining team members and syndicate principals who thoughtfully brought along Moët bubbly. The good times rolled as the cat cruised at 15 knots. Above, John wake raises a magnum as Whidden gives thumbs up and Conner salutes a well-wisher.

At the compound, John Barnitt unleashes a torrent of Moët suds upon Conner and Jerry LaDow (red hat), who don't seem to mind.

Before thousands of cheering supporters at the San Diego Yacht Club, the ceremonial dunking got underway.

Wearing the team colors, Judy Conner celebrates at the compound with other syndicate wives and families. Non-swimmer Dennis (right) keeps a firm grip on the dock during his immersion with the spoils of victory.

Margherita Bottini's double exposure of Stars & Stripes' ghostly image over the press conference illustrates a central issue of America's Cup XXVII: the monohull vs. the catamaran.

A scene from the press conference after Race #1. Between a bemused Tom Whidden and a wary Bruno Trouble, Conner assesses the effect of his response to David Barnes' suggestion he was sand bagging: "When he's won four America's Cups, he can tell me how to do it."

Arch rivals: separated by Australia's Warren Jones, Burnham listens while Fay speaks at the press conference following Race #2. Fay reaffirmed he would seek the court's ruling on the legality of the catamaran.

Post race press conferences were stormy. After Race #1, David Barnes accused Conner of "sand bagging", not sailing as fast as possible. "I guess when he's won four America's Cups, he can tell me how to do it," Conner replied. After Race #2, fur flew as emotionally-heated, insulting exchanges occurred between the two sides. The conduct was generally unbecoming. Given the contentious nature of America's Cup XXVII, anything else would have been a surprise. As *San Diego Union* yachting correspondent Bill Center wrote, "Anyone studying why nations go to war would do well to examine this America's Cup." No one bowed before they came out fighting this time around, and no one shook hands after the match. Because for Michael Fay, the fight wasn't over. Fay was back on dry land, his battleground of preference, itching for the next round.

A few weeks after the racing was over, Dennis Conner put America's Cup XXVII in perspective: "We didn't ask for this match. We didn't concoct it—Fay did. then he said, 'Hey wait, I didn't want you to defend yourselves.' It was an alley fight. He jumped us, and I turned around and decided to fight to the death. I got a little bloody, but kept the Cup. I had a job to do. I could have walked away and let America lose. It was a thankless job, but someone had to do it. Otherwise the Cup would be in New Zealand. I'll let history decide, and I think I'll come out alright."

"We'll all get over the bitterness, and as a result of this challenge, 50 million more people are aware of the America's Cup. In the end, it will have been good for the sport."

THE FUTURE
In Search Of Balance And Equity

by Edward du Moulin

Alan Bond

Even before the races were over, high-level meetings had begun to determine the future course of this habitually storm-tossed trophy. After a summit meeting that included Doug Alford, Alan Bond, Malin Burnham, Michael Fay, Warren Jones, Sail America Trustee William Packer, and New York Yacht Club Commodore Frank Snyder, the San Diego Yacht Club drafted procedures for America's Cup XXVIII. And there was no dearth of rumors involving everything from the formation of new syndicates to the selection of new boats. Whatever else history would decide, America's Cup XXVII was a watershed: big changes were in the offing. Veteran yachtsman and former syndicate manager Ed du Moulin was asked to assess the Cup's future.

Frank Snyder

The venerable 137-year-old bottomless Trophy has survived many crises including civil, world and political wars, and economic depressions.

The world can ill afford to lose events like the America's Cup, events which contribute to national pride, encourage international friendships, advance yacht design, and develop character of young men and women.

It wasn't until the unorthodox and startling challenge of the Mercury Bay Yacht Club in June of 1987, and the continuing saga in court, that the world realized the Deed of Gift had outgrown its traditional role. As long as "mutual consent" is exercised by the challenger and defender, the present Deed of Gift is not only workable, but provides an excellent format for an international competition. However, we know by bitter and costly experience that the lawyers have bared the weaknesses inherent in the present instrument. In particular, the 1887 Deed does not provide a mechanism for dealing with multiple challenges, other than mutual consent.

Constructive dialogue is under way among those representing the yacht clubs which have defended the Cup; namely, New York, Royal Perth and San Diego. Input from countries with long America's Cup traditions—England (where it all started), Canada, France—can guide the San Diego Yacht Club, present trustee, in presenting to the Supreme Court of the State of New York amendments to the 1887 Deed, or a new deed which will insure at least another 150 years of outstanding yacht racing.

An updated instrument may well include fundamental changes:

—clarification of procedures for accepting multiple challenges.

—insurance that matches are held in a recognized class of yacht, or with vessels built to a recognized measurement rule within practical parameters.

—extension of the minimum period between challenges from 10 months to 24 months.

The justification for a review of the Deed is best described in an excerpt from the History of the New York Yacht Club: "The Amended Deed of Gift supersedes the very simply worded original deed of gift which conveyed the Cup to the Club in 1857. The amended deed was designed to eliminate the problems and misunderstandings encountered in the seven challenges from 1870 through 1887".

Currently, there are sufficient and perhaps even more serious problems implicit in the twenty-seventh challenge than those that led to the 1887 amended Deed. Meanwhile, we have witnessed "temporary" measures that hopefully will be incorporated in a new deed.

Sail America Foundation's President Malin Burnham commented that the Deed of gift, properly amended, should result in "multi-national challenges on a level playing field. Each competitor should have the same opportunity to design and build the fastest boat, and to sail her to her fullest potential."

As late as the *Liberty* defense in 1983, the budget of $5 million was criticized as overly large. Some thought it would jeopardize the Cup's future. But the sources of these funds were predominantly individual contributions (90% individual, only 10% corporate).

The glamorous 1987 event in "the land down under" reflected budgets of $15 million with corporations taking a larger role in overall funding than ever before. It becomes clear that in the future the America's Cup must compete for a small share of corporate marketing dollars. The 1988 "aberration"—the multihull vs. the monohull—is a predominantly corporate effort that may well cost Sail America over $10 million.

To be successful, the next defense team will require upwards of $25 million and additional millions will be needed to run the regatta. We will again rely heavily on corporate America. Even the conservative New York Yacht Club in 1980 conceded, though reluctantly, that marketing is essential in today's climate, except for the financial "moguls" (Bond, Fay, de Savary) who can finance their own campaigns.

The Cup is no longer a purely corinthian sports. However, the competition for the America's Cup will still be a contest between recognized yacht clubs, conducted by amateur committees and overseen by highly respected international judges. Thus, like Wimbledon or Henley, it will retain some of the old traditions. On a smaller scale, a Cup defense is similar to the Olympics, where sports and marketing compliment each other.

We can expect more challenges from "token" yacht clubs such as Secret Cove (Canada) and Mercury Bay (New Zealand), dominated by one or several individuals. Challenges won't always come from a yacht club with the traditions and stature of the past and present defending clubs. But "recognized" yacht clubs they must be to conform to the Deed of Gift. And once again these clubs will compete for the Louis Vuitton Cup in the Challenger Trials, and the right to race in the America's Cup finals.

The defender trials which contributed so heavily to the successful American defenses in the past may not play such an important role in the future. The substantial cost of developing a successful defender may force independent campaigns to merge into larger defense groups. Major corporations wishing to have their dollars riding on a sure winner will seek out the most likely winner. This will not prevent smaller groups (such as the Heart of America, Eagle, and Courageous campaigns of 1987) from competing for the right to defend. Such efforts may not end up in the winner's circle, but they will satisfy individual desires, add to the glamour of the event, and contribute to the defense.

It is hoped that the few independently "wealthy" individuals who are willing to put up their own money for larger yachts will not discourage competition from those with more modest funds.

In 1991 we could see the 12 Meters adapted with taller masts and more sail area to meet light air conditions off San Diego, a fling the class surely deserves. If not 12 Meters, we shall witness a new class in the 60-75' LWL range that will stimulate worldwide interest. In either case, we'll once again thrill to a "slam dunk," and 50 or more tacks on a single leg. While still a contest of yacht designers, future Cup matches will again require keen helmsmen and able sailors. When that day arrives we may thank Michael Fay for forcing the America's Cup into the 21st century.

Footnote

The announced resumption of the New Zealand claim to the courts that the catamaran is illegal may write a new chapter to America's Cup XXVII. Whatever the outcome of New Zealand's suit, we must look forward. We must put forth our best effort to make the Deed as equitable as possible for the conditions of modern, multiple-challenge competition. The donors deserve no less than a straightforward and objective updating of "their Deed".

Participants

John Acton Robert Adams Demetrio Aguilar Emilio Aguilar Mario Aguilar C. Douglas Alford Joy Allen Dallas Armstrong Edward Askew Douglas Augustine W. Barry Ault Steve Avedesian Karen Azevedo Ron Azevedo Sue Azevedo Buck Barker David Barker John Barnitt Skip Banks David Barnes Jeff Bason Kerri Beck Stony Beck Chris Bedford Allison Bell Vanessa Bellamy Sandy Benson Dr. Robert Beyster Brian Bilbray Cory Bird Mort Bloom Sean Booth Janet Bording Margherita Bottini Russell Bowler Dr. Sam Bradfield Richard Brassard Daniel Brown Jay Brown J.W. Brown Clive Brown Marcus Brown Paul Brown Carl Buchan Jack Buchanan Jimmy Buffet Ray Burk Malin Burnham Roberta Burnham Doug Byrnes G. Wytie Cable Trish Campbell William Campbell Steve Cantrell Rowena Carlson Maria Carter Leslie L. "Pete" Case Daniel Charles Britton Chance, Jr. Carlos Chovaz Justice Carmen Beauchamp Ciparick Bruce Clark Bill Cleator Robert Cleveland John Clinton Cheri Cloud Graeme Coleman Dr. Wayne Coleman Dennis Conner Judy Conner Elizabeth Copper Del Cover Donald Cowie Robert Crandall Steve Creighton Patrick Curren Tony Dalbeth Lee Davis Rod Davis Ron Davis Peter Debreceny Frederick G. Delaney III Bob DeLong Pietre Denhartog Michael Dingman Gary Distefano Greg Distefano William Dixon, Jr. Teresa Dixson Charles Dominas Mark Dowley Gerald Driscoll Mike Drummond Edward I. du Moulin Thomas F. Ehman, Jr. Jane L. Ellison John Engle James Ensworth Laurent Esquier Peter Eunson Bruce Farr Michael Fay Thompson G. Fetter Barry Feinstein Shelley Fields Maria Flannigan Kim Fletcher Warwick Fleury John Folting John Folvig Tom Ford Daniel Forster Judge Charles W. Froehlich, Jr. Frederick A. Frye Arturo Garcia Fransico Garcia Jose Garcia Pablo Garc Kerry Geraghty Hal Georgens Sheryl Gibson Cy Gillette Patrick E. Goddard Bob Graham John Grant Lesleigh Green Murray Greenhalgh Alan Greenway Lee Grissom Antoine Guerin Rear Admiral Benjamin P. Hacker Stephen Hand Bill Handey Chuck Hansen Jason Harju Terry Harper Marshall Harrington Carlos Harrison Kevin Harrison Mark Hauser Harman Hawkins Keith Hawkins Ramon Hernandez Halsey Herreshoff Rebecca R. Heyl Denise Hill Sheila Hill Kathy Hines Pamela Hom Richard Honey Charles B. Hope Kip Howard Dave Hubbard Andrew Hughes David Hurley Don Innis JJ Isler Peter Isler Peter Jackson Steve Jahn George Jakich Andrea Jankovich Captain Richard S. Jarombek Laura Jefferies Michael Jenkins Peter Jeromson George F. Jewett, Jr. Lucy Jewett Gary Jobson Andrew Johns B.D. Johnston John Karkow Richard Karn Jim Kelly Richard Kendall Mike Kennedy Greg Ketterman Nichole Kezsely Kevin Kinas Paul Kinas Dick Knoth Windie Knoth Patty Krebs Betty Kujawa Jerome LaDow Sally LaDow Lisa Lareau Lyle LaRosh Dan Larsen Kathy Leiber Holly Leimgruber Peter Lester Cam Lewis Hugh Limebrook Lars Linger Pierre LeMaout John Letcher John Leppert Robert Lichter Sally Lindsay David Lloyd Adam Loory Michael Lorelli David Lorimer Gordon Luce Art Lujan Kathy Luther Peter Lynch Duncan MacLane Michael Madigan John Magras Lance Mansen John K. Marshall Paul Matich Rich McCurdy Murray McDonnell Dave McGuigan LaMonta McLarty Gregory McRoberts Kristine Mechtly Andrew Mikesell Mark Millbank Catherine Miller Jennifer Miller Martin Miller Chris Mitchell Tom Mitchell Elaine Mmahat Julie Molstad Matthew Montgomery Dennis Morgigno Gino Morrelli Richard Morris Rubin Muir Jeanette Mullen Michael Munoz Capt.David A. Neal Bruce Nelson Bill Nelson Gil Nettleton Linda Nicholas Bernard Nivelt Kay North Diane O'Brien Maureen O'Conner Clay Oliver Dene Oliver Yarka Ondricek William B. Packer, Sr. Dr. Homer Peabody Jose Perez Darren Peruson Ken Poovey Catherin Powell H.P. "Sandy" Purdon Roland Puton Henri Racamier Francis S. Radford Allen Rapp Tamara L. Rash Marisa Vallbona Rayner John Reid Capt. R.W. "Robin" Reighley Kip Requardt Jim Reynolds Terry Richards James Richmond Chuck Richie Sally Riggs Linda Robinson Steve Roel Ray Roettger Kaysie Rogers Bob Rohloder John Roncz Kirby Ross J.G. Rosson Scott Ruedy Burt Rutan Chris Salthouse Nils Salvesen Julia Sammers Anne Sandison Ken Satterlee John Sawicki Derek Scallet Jeremy Scantlebury Tom Schnackenberg Linda Schneider Michael Schneider William Schreyer Barbara Schwartz Alfred P. Schweitzman Carl A. Scragg, Ph.D. Julie Shepard-Lovell Barry Shillito Alan Smith Dana Smith Mark Smith Randy Smyth Steve Soares Jacky Spencer Jeff Stafford Lee Stein David Stockwell John Stopplemann Jack Sutphen Stephen Talbot Andrew Taylor Thomas Thelen Lisa Thompson Dana Timmer Mark Title George Tomkins Bill Trenkle Marianne Trenkle Gene Trepte Steve Trevurza Bruno Troublé Daniel Tully Dick Turner Harry L. Usher Karen Van Dyke Roger Vaughan Damaso Vega Dory Vogel Scott Vogel John Wake Peter Walker Richard Watts Steven Ward Peter Warren Dal Watkins M.S. Red Webb Lynn Wedel Kenneth Wells Tom Whidden Frank Whitton Rhys Williams Chris Wilkens Peter Wilson Jane Wilson Tom Wilson Steve Woodruff Donn Wuest A.G. Zimba Mike Zuteck

Credits

CONTRIBUTING PHOTOGRAPHERS

MARGHERITA BOTTINI: pages 10, 11, 12, 13, 14, 15, 17, 20, 21, 28, 30, 31, 32 (top), 33 (top), 41 (3), 46, 47 (2), 49 (top), 57 (2), 58 (2), 61 (2-bottom), 62 (2-bottom), 63 (2-middle), 64 (2-top), 65 (2-top/bottom), 66 (top), 67 (top), 68, 71, 76, 78 (top), 84, 85, 104 (2-top/bottom), 105, 107, 108, 109, 114 (Top), 116 (3), 124 (top), 125 (bottom), 126 (2-top), 127 (2-top), 129 (2-bottom), 136 (top), 138 (top), 139 (2-bottom), 140 (top).

DANIEL FORSTER/DUOMO: pages 16, 32 (bottom), 33 (bottom), 34, 36, 37, 38, 53 (top), 56 (2), 75, 124 (bottom), 125 (top), 128, 131, 132, 133, 134 (2), 136 (bottom), 137 (top), 139 (top), 140 (2-bottom), 142 (bottom).

MARSHALL HARRINGTON: front and back covers, end papers and pages 6, 18, 19, 23, 25, 27, 42, 49 (bottom), 51 (2), 54 (2), 55 (2), 60 (5), 61 (2-top), 62 (3-top), 63 (2-top/bottom), 64, (2-bottom), 65 (top middle), 66 (2-bottom), 67 (2-middle), 69, 72, 73 (2), 74 (2), 79, 80, 81, 82, 83, 86, 87, 88, 89, 90, 91, 92, 93, 94, 95, 96, 97 (2), 98, 99, 100, 101 (2), 102, 103 (2), 104 (middle), 106, 126 (bottom), 127 (bottom), 129 (top), 135, 138 (bottom), 139 (top middle), 142 (top).

OTHER CONTRIBUTORS

Sail America · drawing, page 2

Bruce Farr · drawing, page 3

The Washington Post · drawing, page 29
All Rights Reserved, Rosenfeld Collection
Mystic Seaport Museum, Inc.

Acquired in honor of Franz Schneider · page 35

Dan Nerney · pages 39 and 112

J.H. Peterson · pages 43 (2)

Courtesy of Jim Reynolds · page 44

Roger Vaughan · page 44 (bottom)

Yves Rozier · page 53

Cam Lewis · pages 65 (mid-bottom), 67 (bottom), 130 (2), 137 (bottom)

Peter Isler · page 70 (2)

Media Photo Group · page 77

Arthur Krazinsky · page 78 (bottom)

Rob Tucker, Foto Pacific · pages 110, 114 (bottom)

Ockam Instruments · drawing page 117

Laurie Warner · pages 118, 123

Barry Feinstein · illustration page 119

Frank Micelotta/Sports Illustrated · page 119

Barry Feinstein · page 121

EDITORIAL AND DESIGN CONTRIBUTORS

Kip Requardt

Holly Leimgruber

Alfred Schweitzman

SPECIAL THANKS

Eastman Kodak Company

Toshiba America, Inc., Information Systems, Division

Grosvenor Industries

Southern California Lithographics

Toyo Printing Inks and Color Matching · CCS/Toyo Ltd., CA

This book was prepared with duPont materials and proofed with duPont Chromalin®

This book was written on a Toshiba T1200 Portable Personal Computer.